The Heart's Mind

How Unconscious Responses in Life and Work

Naturally Improve Our Lives

While We Make Other Plans

Elizabeth Diane

© 2018 Elizabeth Diane Garcia Martin

Cover Design and Original Art by Grace Powell

Publishing as *The Art of Perspective*
A Perspective LLC
Colorado Springs, CO 80901

Contact by email: aperspective@icloud.com

ISBN-13: 978-1721238569
ISBN-10: 1721238565

(Printed through CreateSpace and for Kindle by Amazon.com, registered with BooksInPrint.com®)

The Art of Perspective:

Our natural inclination is to be happy in work.^{SM}

Table of Contents

Page

One: A Place for Heart in Life   1

Two: The Heart's Mind   3

Three: Historical Relevance   6
        -   The Importance of Relevance

Four: Riding the Train of History: My Story   10
        -   Ground Zero
        -   Back to the Drawing Board
        -   Job as Savior?

Five: The Undaunted Heart   19

Six: Effortlessness   25
        -   Judgment
        -   Value the Individual

Seven: The Source of Strength   30
        -   Equilibrium

Eight: Personal Leadership Styles: A Model   34
        -   Stylistic Leadership

Nine: Natural Systems   39
        -   The Science of Beauty and Simplicity

Ten: Elementary Science   42
        -   Observation
        -   Hypothesis
        -   Test and Correct
        -   Criteria
        -   Why Logic? Why Sequence?
        -   The Sequence of Natural Unconscious Response
        -   Systems and Perception

Eleven:	The Culture of the Self	60
	- The Spirit of Creativity	
Twelve:	A New Way of Working	66
	- A World Unique	
	- Work as Personal Flow	
	- Working Unconsciously Well	
	- Freedom to Create	
	- Perspective: All of Us	
Thirteen:	Bringing Heart to Life and Work	77
	- Start with Heart	
	- Free the Mind	
	- Watch for Fruit	
	- Enjoy the Process	
	- The Road from Inspiration to Reality	
Fourteen:	Self-Renewing Motivation	83
	- A Compass for the Whole Self	
Fifteen:	The Rise of the Human Spirit	85
Sixteen:	Making the Unfamiliar Familiar	88
Seventeen:	Finding the "me"	91
	- Innate Knowledge	
	- You Already Know This	
Eighteen:	"spirit" is Human	96
	- With All My Heart	
	- Let Go and Catch the Drift	
Nineteen:	Flow	103
	- Stress	
	- New Definitions for Living With Spirit	

Twenty: Unconscious Good   110

Twenty-One: The Cycle of Unconscious Response™   113
             -    A Cycle of 12 Phases

Twenty-Two: Principles of the 12 Phases   117
             -    Part One: Owning Change (Phases One
                  through Six)
             -    Part Two: The Good Heart of Life (Phases
                  Seven through Twelve)

Twenty-Three: Time   129
             -    The 12 Phases Over a Lifespan:
                  The Big Picture
             -    A Year Unfolds in 12 Phases

Conclusion   133
Friends and Mentors   135
APPENDIX: A Personal Chronology of Influential Books   139
About the Author   167

DEDICATION

The world of one person is a deep well. Some submerge to depths of themselves beyond the aid of any other person or agency. It could be that some who submerge never come to the surface again. When a person finds her or his own way out of the deepest depths of the psyche, it is an amazing tale to hear. In going into my own "deep" I was greatly encouraged by the stories of these two people and I dedicate this book to any who have the courage to find their way out.

This book is dedicated to people like Martin Pistorius* and Jill Bolte Taylor** who found their way out from where they were buried alive within their bodies and broke through to the open air of "the topside" where their *persons* could be known, once again.

* "Ghost Boy: Escape from a Life Trapped Inside My Own Body" by Martin Pistorius. Introduced in the NPR program *Invisibilia*'s first broadcast on January 8, 2015, "Secret History of Thoughts," at minute 36:09.

** "My Stroke of Insight: A Brain Scientist's Personal Journey," by Jill Bolte Taylor. Dr. Taylor was a victim of a stroke, lost to the world until she appeared again by the skill of her knowledge, applied to her own brain.

INTRODUCTION

This far-reaching study and the way I apply what I learned requires some explanation.

While I used the scientific process to guide my personal investigation into the phenomenon of unconscious response, I had to let go of the process when it came to having others independently test my theory. While I would welcome such a study, I am not a scientist and do not have resources to initiate group studies. This book is just step one.

My hope is that my history will demonstrate how to separate the exterior experience from interior awareness. Writing is the only way for me to introduce my theory—that good is continually manufactured within human nature. This book could be a help for those who want to take hold of their own positive inclinations.

I present my observations of the heart's mind and the natural phenomenon I call *The Cycle of Unconscious Response*™ as part of my life experience. The feedback I get will help me go further in applying this knowledge and creating increasingly valuable tools to offer for everyone's benefit.

Please note: I am not a mental health professional. This is my story and firsthand experience applied to my personal and professional life. I share it to contribute to the shared pool of understanding. This is one perspective.

If the reader experiences inner turmoil as memories stir in the mind, I recommend seeking the help of a professional counselor or trusted friend or partner to manage personal emotion with support.

One: A Place for Heart in Life

The heart does not move in a straight line, in terms of external experience. Externally, we experience life through the five senses that bring information into the mind and body. Internally we process information body and soul; heart and mind. Emotion is a clue to what registers in the heart. But rather than being the emotional effect, the true heart's mind works outward from the human spirit and moves with unerring intelligence toward true good among us and is locked in on its most effective work: unstoppable, self-renewing positive motivation.

Heart drives the self-renewing motivation that compels us to take action to improve our lot in life. The pursuit of happiness is powered by a desire to satisfy the heart. The emotion of happiness is spontaneous and true, even if fleeting, and it keeps the spark of life glowing. What is happiness for one is unlike happiness for another. Each heart builds its world with pieces that link together year by year over a lifetime. This collage of meaning forms vision and holds importance to only one person, the owner of the heart.

Equality of persons, right to life, the authority of liberty, and the pursuit of happiness are all rights that allow us to be self-directed and to live as unique individuals. The right of the pursuit is the freedom to act on opportunity that matches our private motivation, and this right also leaves the burden of consequence to each person according to his or her choices.

The machinery of life supports each person's heart-driven purpose so that the human *spirit*—the core engine of human life—retains its full strength and vigor until its work is done and its time is over. As one of billions of such creatures, each person is a vital element in the survival and glory of humanity as the highest level of worldly existence.

To bring the heart's mind into our worldview alters our perception of how we will live. Our awareness expands to encompass a lifetime in the body and looks further, into the world of meaning and purpose. Being *spirit* at our core, having an understanding of the entire human experience makes daily survival a thing of adventure. With vision and heart motivation, we can see temporal experiences in their true light: as the raw material for the shape of something timeless and powerful. The power that drives the human engine is formed in the heart's mind.

Two: The Heart's Mind

For a few minutes, set aside what we understand by the physical senses: what we see with our eyes, hear with our ears, smell with the nose, taste with the tongue, touch with the hands. Think about how we are impacted by the material world. We love and hate, desire and reject, work and play, have mercy or severe judgment. These are choices and emotions triggered by what is outside of us. Now look inward. Imagine a time when you were impacted by an unexpected event, such as a car accident or a death in the family. It could also be a positive thing: your first meeting with someone who became very important in your life, or the day you decided to launch your dream.

When we are startled in the heart a sequence of responses follow the initial knee-jerk reaction. Once the shock is over, we work the new thing like an oyster works a grain of sand. The heart's mind is that oyster; life is the grain of sand. The intention of the heart's mind is to build a good thing around whatever life throws at us. The heart's mind is logical, sequential, and purposeful. New beginnings play out in our lives gradually; events unfold. This is the logic and sequence of the heart's mind and its effect on our unconscious minds, words and actions:

- Intuition takes over when the unexpected happens. Spontaneous unconscious response carries me through, accessing my "gut" knowledge and natural skill.

- Intention takes hold of gut reactions. My life priorities, already in place, capture my raw reaction and put in order according to my personal values.

- A settled internal position enables me to turn outward again. I find my place in relation to the new situation and the people involved.

- With intuitive self-preservation, I make strategic movements to establish my position in the circumstance so that my identity is secure, not overcome by other personalities or by unfamiliar circumstance.

- Having weathered change successfully, my equilibrium is restored. The new blends with my previous disposition, and life resumes as before.

- Empowered by prevailing over unexpected change, my inner confidence as an individual reaches a new height.

- The personal, internal management of the unexpected has concluded and the work introduced is taken up by the power that brought it. My hands are taken off the work and "life" finishes the work; success is not entirely mine.

- Pride being tempered, I get to work again but there's a

difference. The familiar is behind me, the unfamiliar ahead. I can only wait. My heart expands and pressure increases.

- Finally the tension releases and I am caught up in a commotion. Like a birthing, there is a revealing of a good of mine that others can also see. Like a seed, a concept grew, matured, and brought about a tangible result.

- A calm follows the commotion, and the shape of the result can be assessed. I comprehend this new thing and feel the full impact of it on my life.

- The shape of life as it was before this began disintegrates, and the new pulls into shape. I can long for what used to be and feel a loss, but as I look into what is now in its place there is hope.

- Life is adjusted by the new, more perfect, element of good. It seems such a slight change that I imagine I can go back to the way it was before. But no, this is a new good that is permanent. It rules, in a sense, in place of the ordinary natural thing it replaced.

Three: Historical Relevance

As an advisor and system designer for many years—to small business owners, enterprise visionaries, start-up entrepreneurs, and artists—I found a common thread. It is in the quality of self-renewing motivation in each inimitable personality. It is the quality of individuality, and once I found it in myself, I could recognize it in others.

One of the principles I use in helping people find the best position for their work or to judge the enduring value of a business, is to start with the big picture: historical relevance.

"Historical relevance" is to place us in history, relative to the greatest current trends in society that are unavoidable. By looking at the course of history, we can more objectively see what kinds of occupations are becoming irrelevant and which are on the rise. Because history unfolds gradually, and because we cannot predict the cultural impact of change, this is necessarily a broad observation.

For example, current occupations and business are technology-centric. In a short period of time technology has changed *all* forms of communication, in government, corporations, and small business, to personal communication with friends and family. If a person chooses, she can avoid electronic communication but it is likely that she will not participate in business as an employee or entrepreneur.

If we do not communicate by cell phone or the Internet in 2018, we are virtually irrelevant in the formation of history. Nevertheless, the information that surrounds a person—bank accounts, tax and legal records, health history—is electronically and instantly updated ("real-time") and is accessible on the Internet to persons with the ability to access that information.

In choosing an occupation or starting a business, looking to the future from a historical point of view helps gauge our chances of success. Even if we choose, as some do, to honor the roots of traditional organic society, we should know our place in history as it changes around us. Then we can deal with the particular challenges we face with strength and resolve.

The Importance of Relevance

To be historically relevant, we must take hold of the potential in historic change and let go of what is lost or displaced. For example, if you believe that you can work for a large company for twenty or thirty years and retire with a pension you hold an opinion that is not relevant in this century. The economic crash of 2008 erased the hope and security of millions of people, and the enduring devastation that followed were the fires that forged a Depression-like resilience. In the fires that consumed old authorities, the strength and resolve of the human spirit was released in our souls.

In finding one's value in the new society, we must accept the massive changes to the landscape. To sum up: in the year 2018 the landscape has been rewired with the infrastructure of innovative technology, exciting *tools* for creative pioneers:

- Interpersonal communication through the Internet, cell phones, social media, emoji, and myriad innovative applications ("apps") have changed society.

- We individuals have been keeping our ideas, attaching our names to them, and throwing our hats into the economic ring.

- In the way that blogging went from the chronicles of the mundane to a viable marketing avenue for business, the creative free-for-all has affected corporations. Nothing organic is possible in the artificial "person."

- Individuals have the opportunity to compete with corporations. We are coming out of obscurity with vision and personal power, taking chances to improve the economic and/or social position for ourselves and our families.

- Any person with the freedom of speech and press can give voice to personal opinion in *any* arena by publishing on the Internet through websites and social media.

- The connection between money and humanity may be restored; service to humanity is the principle that sustains an economy, regardless of changes in technology.

The individual-as-a-business presents an opportunity for thousands of people who otherwise had none, and gave hope to those who reached middle age, thereby becoming less desirable as employees in the tech age. Despite the failures, we discovered how to acknowledge and act upon what the heart desires. We have begun to find what we could do with our own hands and wits; things driven by necessity and prompted by love. If the heart does not compel us, we become oppressed by circumstance.

Four: Riding the Train of History: My Story

Ground Zero

After 13 months in Thailand, my 14-year-old son and I were on a plane to Colorado, leaving his father behind with his new life. Back in small-town Colorado, our married daughter and four grandchildren awaited my return.

It was an unexpected turn in circumstances that shattered my worldview. I had a system. I thought my system was succeeding, even if incrementally, year after year in a difficult marriage. In the 26th year, the whole thing collapsed; my system failed. Some call it divorce.

My heart had been set on duty and obligation supported by beliefs in selective dogma and powered by fear. Trust in these unconsciously held "virtues" proved to be a massive failure. Still, in the turmoil, I had experienced God's goodness, firsthand. Now it seemed that the reality of God was the only thing that tethered me to the world.

I define *God* as the force that personally convinces me of love. It is a real and personal connection between what I perceive in my heart and a customized good delivered to my heart. Customization of any system is personal. This process of customized good delivered to my intangible soul is a private faith, and it is supported by the way I experience life. God is a living force that sustains us as spiritual beings living in a material world.

I had reached full maturity, capable of handling so many problems competently, and now had no idea where I had gone wrong. My emotional well-being hung by a thread, and my confidence was severely shaken; I wondered if I would navigate the second half of my life with any success.

Back to the Drawing Board

I could not accept the prospect of building a future that might again end in colossal failure. As surely as each person has a unique signature, I knew God's signature goodness must be in the world, even if I had not yet encountered it. I needed solid, unshakable, reliable, factual wisdom to rebuild upon, something that was self-evident, not merely reasoned to be true. Now, stripped of doctrine and religion, pure spirit awareness made me willing to learn anew.

As in the past, I put my mind to work with faith and looked into the unknown. The questions in the back of my mind teased me until I embarked on the study behind this book. I started with a tenacious silver cord of faith and the basics of the scientific process. This had been a very successful method through which I had gained vibrant health after years of toxicity, took on responsibility for my children's education, and successfully adapted my corporate training to a family business.

Imagine being able to understand what makes us human by tracing random occasions of certainty and determination down to their source. It's tedious work. In my journey, I developed an acute sense of my internal self as separate from what's "out there." Looking out from my heart, I saw how my unconscious actions *intuitively* expressed the certainties in my heart. The specifics of this discovery will unfold in the following pages.

Over the course of six or seven years, from 2009 to 2015, I was immersed in the crucible that forged all the pieces of my life together in the fires of the economic collapse, known as "The Great Recession." I was enveloped in the massive change that unfolded as economic failure persisted.

Back when I entered high school my dad recommended business courses and I took every business course offered. It was an immersion and imprint on my heart. I had natural inclinations toward business work, and adapted to rapid change in technology. I enjoyed any work I did because I made it fit me with improvements of my own design. These lifelong strengths worked within me to form an unconscious sense of direction in work.

My first career was ten years in an electronics manufacturing company. I went from receptionist at twenty to engineering clerk at 25, and when I left at 31 I had been the buyer and materials manager for four years. Those years were formative years as a worker and manager, and I took my business acumen into home-based occupations from peach farming to freelance computer information services and small business development.

After a year in Thailand I felt I was suddenly back at the starting point in the work force. The first job I got through a temp service gave me the opportunity to reinvent myself. The best of all my experience forged a new profession: installing customized versions of corporate business structures in small business. I started a business to serve small business owners. After six years operating on a referral basis, I became discouraged at not having achieved consistent income. I made the break and went back to college to pick up where I left off at 18.

Although my intention was to get a business or computer degree, one was mind-numbingly too familiar and the other required harder math than I was willing to take on. I took advantage of career counseling provided for students and took the Strong Interest Inventory profile. The profile examines a person from six aspects, including recreation and social preferences. In the summary, all six concluded that I should study and pursue a career in art. It was astonishing since I had never done art before.

I signed up for a graphic design degree—a blend of art and computers, I reasoned. But after three-and-a-half years and being accepted in the program, I found I couldn't tolerate computer illustration. It was essentially programming, which I already knew I hated. I bailed, and with the help of a wise advisor created an interdisciplinary degree program in art and writing, submitted it, and it was approved.

The years I spent there, full time and poor, were the best years of my life. I was rebooted through a societal rite of passage. Somehow, me going to college and graduating made me relatable and it seemed people everywhere suddenly "saw" me as if I appeared out of nowhere. I left Western Colorado in 2009 and headed to Denver.

I was in the same position as a young college graduate, but I was in my 50s, and I was clueless about the financial crash of 2008 that happened while I was euphoric in creative rebirth. I moved in tentative yet inspired steps from where I had lived and worked and raised my family, and where work had always found me, to a city where no one knew me. Although my hope was to work among artists, I experienced firsthand the first wave of unemployment following the crash of 2008. In the arts, even volunteers had trouble getting a position.

Friends helped me while I looked for work and I was in Denver long enough to burn up my savings and my old car. I was forced to return to the world of my childhood in Pueblo. Emotionally, I was overwhelmed with a sense of failure. And I was back where I vowed never to return. The only thing that kept me afloat was being surrounded by the things I brought with me, the paintings that reminded me that despite circumstances I really did become an artist.

I had traveled back in time where my mother and eight siblings (seven sisters) retained a culture that, by now, was almost unfamiliar to me after living apart from them as an adult. My mother celebrated; in her heart I was the prodigal daughter come home, a long-lost piece of a puzzle found. I accepted her sincere joy and love. It replaced an old childhood fixation that she was an uncompromising tyrant, ruling over nine children as if we were a pack of wolves.

My independence was tempered by the fact that without all my family, even a shaky new start would have been impossible. Some wondered at—and criticized—my destitute state in middle age after years of productive work. I had failed to look out for myself, it seemed, when they had acquired property and freedom. My value as a person was being tested.

Job as Savior?

Feeling disoriented, disconnected, and destitute, I nevertheless had to remain positive and confident in the hunt for a job. If I had lost heart at this juncture, I might have seen a job as my only hope. To be sure, job as salvation is a contagious emotion in times of high unemployment. But my heart was in the lead, and I was more interested in retaining my ability to navigate the changes in my life course. Perspective, based on higher values, was more important to me.

After nearly a year, it seemed like hundreds of us displaced workers only succeeded in acquiring an occupation in learning the new computerized system of job-hunting. Computers pre-selected candidates for interviews so that only a few out of hundreds of applicants were seen by a human being. I finally left the trenches, looked out from my heart and was immediately hired at a health store chain.

After two years there, learning that all work is the same, and being where I could enjoy co-workers and customers as the best part of working, my heart on ice thawed and began to burn again for independence. By now I was on my own deep in the heart of Colorado Springs, and the cost of the commute irked me. The sacrifice required seemed out of balance for a job that didn't quite cover expenses.

Even though art and writing were my heart's new fire, I knew I had to make a living with business skills. Despite being a city of half a million, Colorado Springs has the heart of a small town—especially after the high-tech corporations left, taking opportunity with them. Meanwhile, I was getting older, "aging out" of the work force. I have an entrepreneur's heart, and I was in danger of the virtual death of entrepreneurship—playing it safe. I knew "safety" in a job, especially at minimum wage, was an illusion.

So while working the job, I volunteered downtown at the Small Business Administration outreach for business startups, SCORE. It was a heart-exercise that brought much relief, and allowed me the joys of creativity and service. During that time, 2010 through 2014, I saw many people who were trying to use a business to replace lost jobs, or who were coming out of retirement to bring more income to their faltering financial situation. The shoes of the corporation were too big for these stalwart, resourceful individuals who were ready to get at it with a lot of heart and know-how, but without a lot of money.

I proposed an outreach and SCORE leadership sponsored a roundtable event I called "Conversations About You as a Business." The idea was to bring advisors, entrepreneurs, and grassroots business owners together as team players to create new game plans. Entrepreneurs brought reports from the field where so much of the business startup world had changed and was still in flux. The modern entrepreneur was leading business development with technology, more so than products. Still, business and economic principles remained the same and institutions were still conservative. Together we surveyed the real problems in the current economic condition. These were interesting times at the dawn of the new economy. We worked with an eye toward survival.

Five: The Undaunted Heart

The heart has a mind of its own. If the heart is denied, that living force is buried alive. It can lie dormant, in a sense, and can erupt unexpectedly through any avenue open to it on the surface. If the heart has so much power—a power that can completely alter what happens on the surface—I decided I would do better if I respected that power. Just as the life force in a plant makes it grow, something in me strained to find light. I learned to stop ignoring my heart's mind and give it a place in my new worldview. I found that simply acknowledging its influence increases my respect for the power of the heart, and gives it a place of importance alongside mind, body, and emotion.

It is difficult to identify and label the thoughts and intention of a heart touched by spirit, but we can be sure of one thing: it will always draw us toward good, like a plant toward the sun.

The bad economy persisted and stubbornly ignored my hopes that volunteering would bring connections that would lead to a good job. The financial fires stoked increasingly higher, peaking for me in 2012. Encouraged by my fellow advisors at SCORE I attempted a business again, marketing and technical support for the "not-just-for-profit" business builder.

Just as I thought I was gaining traction, wildfires raged in the mountains around Colorado Springs and to everyone's horror the fire galloped over hills and down into affluent neighborhoods. When it was over, 346 homes had been destroyed. I could feel a paralysis settle over the city. People I had begun to work with in small business and startups became emotionally paralyzed, withdrawing to protect what they had as if a new fire would blaze and get them. My business launch was aborted.

To regroup, once again my heart drew me toward the place where motivation never failed. Still leading the roundtable events, I dared to bring into the world of strictly business my discovery of unstoppable, self-renewing motivation as the source of industry. I asked each advisor to join me in sharing what it is that drives us to serve, and I asked the people in the business group to each share why they started their businesses. It was a little awkward at first, but the mood began to change as people connected to the reasons why their work centered on what gave them great personal satisfaction.

This inspired me to continue bringing this message wherever I went. I began talking about something so irrelevant in the business world, and yet so essential to living well as workers. Speaker Simon Sinek talks about the *why* of a business; I was talking about the why in the individuals *behind* the business. Every time I said with trepidation that I help people realize their own self-renewing motivation by recognizing unconscious response—*every* time—the person I spoke to wanted to hear more.

Now traction was happening beyond my own success with my theories. My excitement grew along with my increasing confidence. With each new conversation, I learned to describe my work a different way. This was not a business venture; it was a tangible breakthrough for my life's work. I was finally able to bring my odd contribution into interaction with others, and it actually had a positive effect! Still, for others it was a long way from the heart to the head.

My "crazy," as I call it, was essentially *doing my thing* in every situation by keeping action closely connected to my heart. Artists are the perfect model for this way of working. I developed the model with integrity since I now fully understood the work of an artist and the heart of the entrepreneur. *Creativity* and *innovation* are different words for the same internal process, one that ends in the same vibrant outcome: a new product for public consumption.

All of it harmonized with my study of the silent energy that moves us to pursue the vision in our hearts, to be on that path in any way possible. I realized that we create the work we love to do, and it often becomes a business. It's the love of working that is the spirit of entrepreneurship, not the money. Compensation, or a trade of equal value, is just a way to balance the two.

It took a lot of guts but when all other options closed up, doing my thing was the *only* thing I could do. It was where my motivation was highest, and I had the energy, knowledge, and ability to work, and my "market" was receptive. The path of my own business was proof that a business really can grow naturally from a heart-driven desire and move organically outward step by step. The model became a natural resource that needed some work so that others could use it, and I needed more exposure to test the market, to see what form would work best for others.

I love the innovation and creativity process, mainly because individuality is a principle that attached itself to me at an early age. My seven sisters and I often heard, "You all look alike!" By the time I graduated from high school, I was pushing against time to get out of town and start making a difference. True entrepreneurship requires that a person step out on their own, and be willing to take the hits of nonconformity. Something original, by its very nature, is not immediately recognized, and in the information age new ideas sometimes don't have a physical product.

Breaking new markets was not new to me. I spent years educating my clients about custom workflow processes for small business. Even though my clients were happy with what I did, I couldn't make a consistent income. My service didn't have the same sound and feel as the consultant professionals they either couldn't afford or were unable to conform to in spirit. I had also assumed that my value was apparent, and that clients would hire me for the ability to contribute at a high level.

Now, in this new venture my inner engine rebooted on its own with a surge of renewed power from a source of initiative deeper than my analytical mind had ever gone. I found it when I followed the electric pulse that came from my heart out to my mind and body. Now mind and body happily responded to this internal force, rather than being prodded and pressured to work by forces outside of me.

These are natural forces that work together for our good:

- While we make plans in a straight line, life is a zigzag.
- Life wins over plans.
- Life makes room for love—all kinds of love—while we learn perfect love.
- Physics and biology might restrict our progress. Some things we dream are redirected by limitations of materials or our physical ability or inability. The heart will find its way regardless of physical constraints.
- Money has to be available to facilitate progress on a dream but the imagination is always working.

- Success cannot be achieved without connection and service in society. Slowing down allows us to build vital connections.

Timing and the convergence of these forces dictate when, in what way, and how fast we pursue our dreams. We only have to manage our expectations with regard to time. Working with the natural rhythm of time and the cycles of life can ease stress; we grow more sure of our way if it harmonizes our whole life.

Six: Effortlessness

Strength is drawn from within. Every person is strong in a unique way, based on his or her winding path of life from birth to the present. Sometimes strength is apparent; sometimes it's only seen clearly in a crisis. True strength is natural and effortless; a product of a person's inner, often unspoken, certainty about what is true.

Strength is something we often take for granted when it is effortless. *What* we do does not show our strength as much as *how* we do things. The way you do a task and the way you relate to people carry a signature—a sign of your identity, as unique as your handwriting. Your strength is as much 'you' as your features or your name. It is natural, and it is indistinguishable from you as a person. You don't plan to *do* strength, like a performance. It shows up in your unconscious, automatic response in a situation.

Once a thing is done, we see the result, or hear appreciative comments from others, and the positive reinforcement creates a connection in the conscious mind. *Then* we can know our own strength when it wasn't known before. We learn what our strengths are intuitively. Strength comes from the way that life allows you to succeed. It's in the way things come to you without you paying the price for it that others pay. It is your unique personal gift, one that came with you at birth. It could be something as simple as the "gift of gab." Those of us who do not have that gift, know it's a gift. The ability to engage someone else in interesting conversation, effortlessly, is a gift. The person who has that gift may protest that it was definitely something they worked on, but they worked with it as raw material. You do not create a personal trait you are born with.

Judgment

The ability to recognize both the faulty and deceitful in life, as well as to detect unearthly, perfect good, makes us human. We soon get past the childhood trust in face value and we learn, in our hearts, to search a thing to its core. This unconscious ability can add much to balance the physical-dominant information we take in. Some people actually know that their "gut instinct" is the best compass in navigating confusing situations.

We may completely overlook how intangible, unconscious and constant perception increases our strength in coping with life. The senses, the physical, our emotions – these can dominate our thinking so much that there's no room for the insight unconscious wisdom can add in judging the physical. The natural ability to detect enduring good, beneath and above the physical, sustains our will to live and it is worthwhile to pursue an intellectual understanding of intangible human powers.

Our ability to detect truth must mature. Initially, if a thing pleases us, we may say we love it, or that it's "good." When what pleased us fades, and we see its inability to truly sustain goodness, we want to fix or discard the thing. Sometimes we discard people because they don't please us anymore, and sometimes the process of maturity helps us realize the difference between sincerity and insincerity, or between honest mistakes and subtle intentional harm.

To get the biggest benefit out of a gift you're born with, accept it with humility and use it to do good. The only reward of a selfish use of a natural gift is in the material, the sensual. But the best thing to be gained out of selfless effortless strength is love—love of life; love for humanity; loving what you do; and best of all, to love and be loved.

The greatest and universal human strength that we all have is the power to judge a thing as to its true merit. We love the good. A physically strong person must be gentle, not mean, if he is to be loved. An intellectually strong person must be motivated by love, if she is to be loved. If the work we do is to be appreciated and rewarded in some way—if someone is to love the way we do things—that way must be of service to someone besides us.

And yet, the only way to be of service in our own unique way is to first discover the value of a thing by its benefit to ourselves. A search into the intangibles of life, and how they are rooted within each of us, will increase confidence in the value of what we contribute in our corner of the world.

As we allow the fourth aspect of humanity to have a place in our thinking—spirit, added to the physical, emotional and intellectual—we increase the occasions of high personal competence and high personal satisfaction in everyday life.

Value the Individual

In the realm of history, we all hold a place, and the value of each unique person is the basis of human dignity. Freedom and self-reliance will restore the value of the individual in the twenty-first century. Each person makes a unique contribution in her and his corner of the world; a purpose that is recognized by the people around her. To undervalue the individual is to undermine the greatest positive source of societal and economic renewal. The vital connection between the human and the machine of business is at the core of this writing.

Business relies on the productivity of individuals and groups—of people. In economic and regional crises, we have watched the collective failure of agencies, politics, courts, and corporations. If we relied on those leaders to solve our personal problems, we soon learned that they have left us on our own. Being left on our own can be a bit of a shock, initially. For some in the wake of the financial disaster in 2008 there was no recovery, and the homeless population grew. When left to our own devices, quite surprisingly, we found we actually have devices to use. The engines of society and commerce started up again when the hearts of people strengthened enough to work for our own benefit. We had to face the fact that no one would save us. We are a new generation of bootstrap economic pioneers.

Seven: The Source of Strength

Inner strength grows through a process of maturity; it has a natural life cycle. Wouldn't it be something to learn how strength comes from within, how we gain strength in maturity?

Anything that repeats is a system, so we can find the purpose or product of an unfamiliar system by observing its repetitions. As the system becomes familiar its intention can be inferred. To find the strength of the human spirit, we must look into the heart.

To understand the system and order of the human spirit—to know its nature, our nature—we must see it within ourselves. This is the method I used to bring these conclusions to my audience. I followed the sequence backward, from impulses of involuntary action that forced me to draw breath to the first movements within my heart and mind. Once I found the fountainhead, the source in my heart, I began to observe the first evidence of what *spirit* initiated and followed it from the inside to the eventual manifestation. I found the heart's *mind*: Agenda, logic, intention, and systematic execution.

By following the natural sequence of the subtle evidence within me, I let the system teach me its intention over and over again. I was startled to find that this system—whose origin is still unknown to me, and whose actions are now familiar and predictable—manufactured one product: good.

I became a willing student to learn how to yield to this process so that I might increase the occasion of good in my life—possibly to encourage the speed of "manufacture" by aiding rather than impeding its progress. I dropped everything; this grew from a search into a way of life.

Equilibrium

We are complex creatures—a mystery of simultaneous abilities in intellectual, emotional, physical, and spiritual forces. We are gyroscopes inside, bringing all the forces together so that we stay upright, holding equilibrium inside, separate from the changes outside.

It is a good thing that our bodies and minds function without us directly managing how they function. The heart pumps blood without us choosing it. We breathe automatically. Our minds dart this way and that, processing a variety of responsibilities and choices. Our emotions pop up freely and unexpectedly, and we often look outward at what provoked them not understanding *why* we are provoked.

Spiritually, our essence is always present and is undetected by physical senses. But there is a way to investigate spirit. We can use secondhand evidence—what comes straight from the heart and out of the mouth. Or, as an artist does, go straight to the hands and begin to make something guided by inner vision.

Being in flow, where all your capacity is engaged in the task at hand, to the point where you lose connection with time and your surroundings—this is the place where you are most capable and most satisfied. We may not understand what is happening when we begin to create, but it shows itself to us as we create it.

We're meant to understand the times when we are in flow. Knowing what conditions invite the opportunity for competence can increase the frequency of a sense of accomplishment and satisfaction.

Many self-help books work on mindset, cultivating a perspective that leads to extraordinary thinking. One of my favorite books is the highly influential "7 Habits of Highly Effective People" by Stephen R. Covey. Covey observed that effective people first master themselves and then move outwardly to have public victory, always expanding their personal growth, "sharpening the saw."

Heart is implied in Covey's first three habits for gaining private victory before going public. You begin by affirming and taking initiative toward your personal vision. Next, see the end from the beginning. Know the straight line from the inner guidance of your highest ideals as you look out toward action. The third habit is to put first things first, beginning with the more difficult, the more satisfying objectives based on principles, not being distracted by busy work or that of gaining something of lesser quality. The whole process works from heart to mind and body.

Long recognized as the woman's domain, heart was overlooked in 20th century business, even though women fully participated in the business arena. In the 21st century the dominant male way of working is making room for the feminine tendency to nurture and sustain relationships. If we advance a win-win philosophy (Covey's fourth habit) and the fifth habit to "seek first to understand, and then to be understood," the way of the heart might get its turn.

The process of mutual understanding fosters Covey's sixth habit, "synergy," where the parties equally contribute to something greater than would occur working separately. One way to reach that harmony is by understanding the heart's mind, which draws on both feminine and masculine traits. As we exercise this new idea, we sharpen our mental "saws" (the seventh habit) to learn new ways of working together.

Eight: Personal Leadership Styles: A Model

Extraordinary thinking can spring from a person's unique self-culture and each type of contribution brings value to leadership. To include all types of people in leadership I devised a personality profile model using heart, mind, soul, and body as characteristic styles. *Heart* and *mind* tend to be oriented to the intangible world of motivation and abstract concepts, *Soul* and *Body* to the tangible world of relationship and activity.

On the surface, a person's self-culture can take on different forms in these leadership styles. Intentions can be made known through words and/or actions, and the style is the way in which communication is carried out. The difference in style shows up in the predominance of one: heart, mind, soul, or body. The "Personal Leadership Style" model assigns a general style to each, as a trait or "style":

- Heart as intuitive (natural and insightful)
- Mind as intellectual (reasonable and specific)
- Soul as emotional (diplomatic and social)
- Body as physical (animated and dynamic)

Think of *heart* as a right-brain (fluid) function and *mind* being a left-brain (strategic) function. Together they complement each other, alternating perspectives on a situation. From the heart, a person considers and applies the transcendent values of fairness and mutual good. The mind would consider the most direct and efficient way to perform a thing. Once heart has established a view beyond the material, the will is resolute, and when the mind has a plan, the applicable physical functions can be executed. Heart and mind may trade positions leading intuition in a situation, with will and action following behind.

In general, a person may be more strongly motivated by one trait over the others and therefore, will take independent spontaneous direction (leadership) in a way characterized by that style. The purpose of this system is to help recognize and clarify deeper motivations that cause us to move toward a highly personal goal, and to recognize differences that become evident in our own spontaneous movements or restraint. The history of one's self-culture drives his or her beliefs about life and what we think is attainable toward those heart-driven goals. Obstacles often rise in relationships, in work, and in the course of life. How we move forward reflects our natural preference for relating to new situations, and in dealing with others.

Stylistic Leadership

The descriptions below of each style may help to identify your strongest personal preference among the basic characteristic of heart, soul, mind, and body. The unconscious choice—on the fly—of one characteristic over the others may indicate connection from the *spirit* of a person's self-culture to how it is *expressed.* Based on the circumstance and according to a person's nature, we impulsively resort to logic or emotion or get busy to maintain control. Through these generalizations we can get a rough idea of how we shift in a natural, fluid manner in response to the myriad and constantly changing circumstances that fill a day. Even though you might identify with all of them in some way, there may be one that best describes your leading inclination.

Consider your internal response to these descriptions. How do you identify, or not identify, with each one?

- ❖ Characteristics of *mind* in leadership:
  - o Primarily motivated by logic and need lots of information before deciding.
  - o Needs time to analyze and hesitates to take action until analysis is done.
  - o Has a strategic position from which to work, according to all available information, and already considered the best place to operate in the sequence of things.
  - o Reduces a problem to facts, converting persons, circumstance and emotion into factors.
  - o Looks for order and create order mentally, within a sphere of influence.

- ❖ Characteristics of *body* (the physical) in leadership:
    - ○ Primarily motivated to stay in charge.
    - ○ Ready to do whatever it takes to stay in charge using words, strength, emotion, money, or whatever, depending on the circumstance.
    - ○ Tends to be the first to take action and direct people.
    - ○ Looks for activity and gets to the front of the line.
    - ○ Gets things done now, unconcerned with underlying reasons.

- ❖ Characteristics of *soul* in leadership:
    - ○ Primarily motivated to be in contact with others.
    - ○ Has great depth of feeling and is happiest in conversation, connecting with people.
    - ○ Looks for outward expression of other people's interests or desires to be able to enter in where others are.
    - ○ Loves doing things with people and readily responds to invitations, rather than be alone.
    - ○ The only objective is to share the moment.

- ❖ Characteristics of *heart* in leadership:
    - ○ Primarily led by intuition and works on vision with personal authority.
    - ○ What we do is entirely apart from what other people do.
    - ○ Sensitive to unexpressed thoughts and feelings of others with minimal interaction to retain objectivity and vision.

- o Needs time to adjust frame of mind before entering in new situations.
- o For the sake of the vision, promotes cooperation among the people involved.

Each of us is naturally capable in all four strengths. As we appreciate various leadership styles, we can allow others to contribute, and we gain a more complete understanding of the whole. A balance of authority and effectiveness comes from the multiplicity and diversity of insightful contributions. Wise leaders value the perspective of those who take time to strategize for long-range outcomes as well as those who excite activity by their drive to take immediate action. We can give room to the leadership of those who bring people together in harmony, and for those who hold the vision and inspire toward ideals.

Nine: Natural Systems

Systems are sequences of activity or motion that repeat, over and over, to accomplish some end. Unconscious activity must be observed over long periods of time before any pattern or sequence can be perceived. It is activity without intellectual intention, and yet it is intelligent and purposeful.

We can follow many natural systems: the sequence of plant growth from the seed to the stem to the flower; the sequence of growth for a fruit tree, from seed to sapling to leaf and flower, eventually to the fruit. Obstetric science discovered the details of veiled activity in the womb, how an embryo develops to a fully formed baby. We now know the phases of the baby's progress and can anticipate the arrival of the baby.

Once a sequence is detected, the relationship of steps in that sequence becomes important: what comes first, next, and so on, until the end is reached. The first step indicates direction and each step is a naturally relevant to the one that precedes it. All steps or phases work together as a whole, each contributing a feature until the whole is attained.

I often find that a surface problem is a symptom, evidence of a systemic problem. This is often how I solved business problems. By separating symptoms from systems we found where we may have unknowingly violated the optimal flow of business operation. As we move from the surface, skimming past everything that works fine, we find root causes and where the separation occurred. Once identified, the irregularity can be adjusted and then the whole process can resume a smooth rhythm.

It took me years to understand the difference between symptoms and the root of a dysfunction in all the factors that contribute to physical health, and I experienced the benefit of healthful habits. In most cases, I found that I had unwittingly thrown a disruption into the design of a healthy body. I learned to remove obstacles to good digestion, correct unconscious slumps and ways of walking that caused pain. I also learned that obsessive discipline in the physical could have a negative impact on health. Focusing on one aspect of health can throw off the optimal balance of the whole person. Once I realized that symptoms were a cry for attention to systemic problems, I became dedicated to maintaining physical, emotional and intellectual health.

The Science of Beauty and Simplicity

In the spiritual, habits I practiced for years and believed were taking me to a good end took me somewhere I did not intend at all! This could only mean that I was again unknowingly violating some optimal design.

The way of the scientist has always interested me. By simply peering into nature, we can learn so many things about ourselves. I learned from science that beauty and simplicity are most often found in nature. Later, in art school, I learned that beauty and simplicity are key characteristics of successful designs. One of the best books I ever read is "The Double Helix: A personal account of the discovery of the structure of DNA" by James D. Watson, co-discoverer of the structure of DNA with Francis Crick. When Watson and Crick finally figured out the right functional structure, they decided it was "too pretty not to be true."

Ten: Elementary Science

Early on, I was emotionally numb. And then, in a random conversation with a friend, a shock of electricity jolted me and words fell out of my mouth from my heart. Afterward I was physically and mentally shaken. The dead calm returned, but here was a sign of life that I did not conjure up. Now I had something real to investigate; I had to find out what happened. Using my mind's eye, I traced the sensation back, from being shaken to the moment of impact.

Observation

Even though the connection between spirit and heart is elusive, there is an effect on the mind that shows up in spontaneous unconscious reactions. Using introspection and a keen physical sensitivity, it is possible to follow the movement from spirit to heart, and into the intellectual, emotional and physical senses.

In rejecting the destructive "knowledge" from my life before, my heart was unmoved by meaningless automatic and necessary activity. It was easy enough to perform the necessary functions by rote: obtaining work to pay bills, cooking, cleaning, maintaining personal hygiene and health, and attending to the needs of my teenage son. Years of habit kicked in and did not require heart initiative, yet I lacked the motivation that previously invigorated and inspired me.

The jolt that briefly started my heart up again occurred when this friend dropped by unexpectedly. Quite the talker, she seemed to have no other purpose than to unload her life drama and the grief she was experiencing in a second marriage. She wasn't a close friend, and I had no particular interest in her woes, having my own to contend with. While I politely half-listened, there came a moment when I realized she had asked me a direct question and was waiting for my answer. This was the moment that triggered my spontaneous response, an impromptu answer that sprang out of my private musing. She was quiet when I spoke, paused to consider what I said, checked her understanding with me, and then, seeing I had no more to say, she resumed her chatter, brought the one-sided visit to an end and left.

In tracing back, I discovered that the jolt was a result of that pause and her question. I realized that the impact that enlivened my heart was in having the attention and respect of another person, in her implied determination to seek me out, to directly obtain my opinion, and to take it in. This was an experience that fed my destitute heart and soul.

It would be months before that kind of experience happened again, where a random electric jolt started my heart beating again. This time it was a chance encounter with the young son of family friends. Although I was nearly shunned by friends and acquaintances who must have detected the dark cloud that surrounded me, this young man seemed unaffected by the change in my circumstances or in *me*. He was working in the grocery store where I was getting a few things, and he greeted me with openness and in the joy of innocent familial affection.

This time, I was shaken immediately and knew this was a source of positive energy, feeding my still-lifeless heart. Now I had a thread, a second "beat" to link to the first. From these two experiences, my mind came alive with curiosity and it began the search that nearly twenty years later produced this theory.

Continuing forward, the intervening years were consumed in the cycle of the scientific process, primarily observation. I would record my feelings and self-observations. I developed objectivity; the feelings were gone days or weeks later, and I could evaluate the progression of attitude. Observation led to an idea and I began testing the idea.

Hypothesis

The three-step pattern rose above the circumstantial details: an unexpected impact; recovery and evaluation; and then internal positioning toward the situation. My conclusion was that these were unconscious responses that are not determined by the slow intellectual process, but were automatic. This showed an intention and logic that arose from some part of my brain.

Daily, for months, I checked this sequence. When I was caught off-guard and reacted, I reviewed the thought sequence by which I recovered. I began to identify singular characteristics of each phase and how they differed from each other.

a.   The impact of something unexpected:

This could be meeting someone for the first time, or having a familiar person radically change the way they interacted with me, as happened in the situations with the two friends previously described.

Much of my reaction had to do with what I expected, life as I knew it, and the fact that what happened is definitely *not* what I expected. The event triggers a gut reaction. Sometimes I would freeze. Other times I laughed or cried without knowing why. There were times when I physically moved away because of the discomfort.

I was doing nothing but surviving when I felt threatened or confused, or showed emotion as a reflex, not a deliberate choice.

b.   Recovery and evaluation:

Shaking off the impulse that had me in its grip, next I would automatically find a place of intellectual calm and restore internal order. This meant sorting. What just happened? Why did I react that way? Was my behavior reasonable, according to the way I want to behave? Did my words or actions embarrass or please me? Sorting through the pieces of the situation, and judging how I reacted and felt helped me grow. Separated from the routine and rote, these occasions revealed things about myself that were new to me; undiscovered. I was engaged in a process that isolated the dynamics of new situations, including my reactions, and by contrast I saw my personal priorities more clearly. I realized that I *have* an internal compass that operates on its own and draws me toward stability.

c.   Internal positioning toward the situation:

Once the sorting was done, I observed that my perspective turned outward again. Now I had a position of my own, separate from the people and situation that impacted me. I could find a place outwardly where I could reside safely. Sometimes this meant that I could not accommodate a person or a request without violating what I felt as a safe position, the position of my authentic person.

I made choices; internal determinations not shared with anyone. In rebuilding my life these choices were a matter of personal survival, a basis where functions were still attached to my heart.

The hypothesis indicated a power that electrified my otherwise mechanical living. If unconscious responses led me to self-preservation, with intention, independent of intellectual choice, and if that direction was positive, this could be a key to having the fullness and meaning I so needed in my life.

Test and Correct

I began to share the idea randomly and ask people if they felt that the three-step internal process was also their experience. People generally acknowledged it was so. One time a man thought it through and said, "Yeah. So what?" He had no idea how it encouraged me that he accepted my initial discovery and hypothesis as so self-evident as to be unimportant.

After a year or so, my habits became fixed inside of these boundaries. As the three-step pattern settled in the back of my mind I perceived a slight expansion, a natural next step. New situations gave me occasions for personal growth. Having a secure internal position, I could move into new situations differently by choosing words and actions carefully to anchor my personal priorities in a new way.

A resolve close to the heart is unstoppable and I found that others are willing to accommodate my forward motion if they feel no conflict with their own position. I was not in opposition to others; I was nurturing and protecting my true self and ensuring the continuation of that heart-driven, living force. If any difference arose, my tenacious determination, even if unspoken, would ensure that I was not run over by stronger forces. I did not presume to know what was to come next.

The whole experience had the effect of breaking through barriers and attaining a new level of personal growth. So I was surprised by the subtlety in the next phase: relaxation. The struggle ended and balance returned and I could feel a private celebration. This was an accomplishment no one knew as intimately as me.

Now it was back to work as usual, but with new strength and skill. Breaking through to success is exhilarating. On a straight course toward my objective, it seemed nothing could stop me. But then the "fifteen minutes of fame" height ended abruptly. Not the glass ceiling, but life happens. There are no super humans who get it all. Of course.

More months of observing and testing confirmed these additional phases and I became very excited about the hidden world now revealed to me. But this was only preliminary observation and conclusion. I had to continue to utilize the scientific process to follow to its end the vein of unintentional personal growth, coming from deep within.

Criteria

I continued to test, and developed a set of criteria. Observations of this internal reflex must be tested with an intention to exclude personal and cultural bias:

- Gender. This was a study of the innate spark of human motivation, not based in anatomy, physiology, or any lifestyle that could be identified as springing from anatomy, physiology, or lifestyle.

- Nationality. I had been separated from the homeland for over a year, and lived off the tourist track on one that skimmed over the top of the Thai culture. This broke the continuity I had in Colorado and I returned with a kind of objectivity about American culture as a whole. The nature of people is human.

- Age. I found a basis of common identity and simple human affinity, regardless of age. As a parent and grandparent, I found it impossible to connect with a child's broken heart and maintain discipline using an authoritarian manner. Necessity demanded deeper communication to understand a child's unique form of grief. I found the same emotional and physical reflexes in children as I have as an adult: the aching in the gut while crying, for example. Children do not yet have words for grief.

- o A few years after I returned to America, my family went through the difficult process of restoration. Our new family unit consisted of my recently divorced 30-year-old daughter, her four young children (ages 6-10), my then 18-year-old son, and me. While the study went forward, it became extraordinarily important to encourage love and each one's desire to be part of a family unit again. In a highly emotional and unhappy circumstance, we had to find the highest and best natural motivation for each of us.

- Eastern and Western spirituality. The influence of Eastern mysticism, even in small-town Colorado, was more noticeable to me after living in Buddhist Thailand. But in the west we use Eastern religion and philosophy without the Buddhist devotion, temples and shrines. My search was increasingly focused on the natural human phenomenon. Even if a spiritual principle is understood in Eastern mysticism, I wanted to express what I found about the heart and spirit in my native Western logic and language. In other words, if this is an observable natural phenomenon of human nature, it was not necessary to use labels adopted from Eastern culture and language.

- Christian religious doctrine. I had read the entire Bible at least three times and had done studies and analyses, in context, independently for years. Once free, I realized that self-preservation was a strong influence on what I once believed to be faith and that study was a way to be validated. Aside from the personal faith I retained, the search for spontaneous positive motivation was quasi-science so I learned to separate natural spirituality from religion.

America is not a spiritually-oriented culture, as Thailand seemed to be, but Christianity is imbedded in our culture and language. So occasionally I allowed a reference that was common and implicit in Western society because of Christianity. The "Sabbath" to indicate a day of rest, is one example, or the Bible story of Israel's exodus out of slavery. In fact, the Exodus is a great analogy for the release from cultural and religious views that don't necessarily promote the well-being of the spirit.

My search was for something in the unaltered human spiritual function that knew how to find good. It was a study to quantify primitive evidence of a *reliable* good that is not a product of human reasoning or conscious deduction.

Like a scientist, I was observing a heretofore-unknown (to me) natural activity. My own unplanned, spontaneous words and actions caught my attention because they had the force of life, but I had not exerted conscious effort—the kind of effort that everything else demanded of me.

The product of a system often indicates the purpose and value of the system. As I built my new life around invigorating and spontaneously productive thoughts and motions, my confidence about my future grew strong. I now believe that life manufactures good as methodically and consistently as an apple tree manufactures its leaves and fruit.

Why Logic? Why Sequence?

I set forth this discovery: a system that naturally and automatically manufactures good. To recognize a natural experience as a system, it is important to see the phases as a sequence that moves logically toward a particular outcome. In a sequence we use numbers to keep each step in a position relative to the whole. In this system there is a sequence of twelve phases where each operates individually around a principle.

One way to perceive the 12 phases as a whole is in the way we experience a whole year naturally, day by day, in the passing weeks, months, and as season change. A whole year unfolds and yet we rarely see the whole year at once except in retrospect.

That natural rhythm is what I also found in the 12 phases of unconscious response and, in retrospect, recognized logic in the way each phase is connected to those before and after it. Once I brought the phases together a design appeared. The challenge was to find language to describe what I saw.

The Sequence of Natural Unconscious Response

Each phase is an experience that performs a specific function, and is also a contributing part of the whole design. The whole design reveals its purpose in the end result, but each experience stands on its own. This is the way I describe the natural sequence of unconscious response:

1. Intuition takes over when the unexpected happens. Spontaneous unconscious response carries me through, accessing my "gut" knowledge and natural skill.

2. Intention takes hold of gut reactions, and my life priorities, already in place, subdue raw reaction within personal values.

3. A settled internal position enables me to turn outward again. I find my place in relation to the new situation and the people involved.

4. With intuitive self-preservation I make strategic movements to establish my position in the circumstance

so that my identity is secure, not overcome by other personalities or by unfamiliar territory.

5. Having weathered change successfully, my equilibrium is restored. The new blends with my previous disposition, and life resumes as before.

6. Empowered by prevailing over unexpected change, my inner confidence as an individual reaches a new height.

7. The personal, internal management of the unexpected has concluded and "life" takes over. My hands are taken off the project that I saw as only mine, and the work of others comes in without regard to "my" project. it is clear that success is not entirely up to me and I receive benefits I did not work for.

8. Pride being tempered, I get to work again but there's a difference. The familiar is behind me, the unfamiliar ahead. I can only wait. My heart expands and pressure increases.

9. Finally, the tension releases and I am caught up in a commotion. Like a birthing, there is a revealing of a good that others can also see. Like a seed, a concept grew, matured, and brought about a tangible result.

10. A calm follows the commotion, and the shape of the result

can be assessed. I comprehend this new thing and feel the full impact of it on my life.

11. The shape of life as it was before this began disintegrates, as the new reveals its shape. I can long for what used to be and feel a loss, but as I look into what is now in its place there is hope.

12. Life is adjusted by the new, more perfect, element of good. It seems such a slight change that I imagine I can go back to the way it was before. But no, this is a new good that is permanent. It rules, in a sense, in place of the ordinary natural thing it replaced.

This sequence of twelve movements reveals the expansion of good in some minute form. This good can only be perceived, not understood. The change is incremental, and I can follow its progress just as a botanist can follow the emergence of a plant, or a gynecologist can determine, at any particular point in time, what phase of development a baby is in the womb.

I realize how incredible this sounds, that I was able to "watch" the progress of good through the internal unconscious response and follow it out to an occurrence on the surface. I feel compelled to report what I discovered just the way I found it. I conclude that there are twelve distinct phases of the path of good deposited in the heart, and that the inner response changes me in an elemental way, so that my whole being leans toward the good. Good *feels* good and it is natural to the human spirit to accept and nurture that good.

Systems and Perception

Characteristics of the movements formed principles that guide me in judging my subjective thoughts and conscious decisions. I sense the rhythmic progression and I direct my mind toward it. Once I pinpoint the principle for the time in which I stand I align my mind, emotions, and actions to follow the principle. It is a heart repositioning, where otherwise I would naturally miss the point of the function.

As my life and work became centered on natural spontaneous drive, and as old habits by rote fell away, I began to work with *life*. And then it seemed that life itself began to work with *me*.

Getting back into the work force wasn't difficult, at first. I was hired quickly through a temp agency, and that employer soon hired me full time. It was a basic office job for a high-end interior design company. I was expected to stay behind the scenes and not interfere with the busy company, especially the staff of designers. I mistakenly thought it was just a pretty and fun place to work. It wasn't long before waves of intensity in the place rippled my way. Everyone was on edge.

No one seemed to know or care what I did; they just didn't want to be bothered with the constant phone calls. The business manager was apparently instructed to keep me from talking to the owner and head designer, even though I was technically her assistant. His job was to screen messages and questions for her and take care of anything that didn't absolutely require her attention.

So I watched and learned. I was also the design resources librarian, which didn't seem to entail much more than putting books and samples back or inserting updates. I felt responsible when the owner became frustrated that she couldn't find a particular item in the library. She had to look through a few catalogs and would usually find that someone had misplaced the item. Case by case, I could put things where she wanted them but her needs were a mystery to me.

After a few weeks, her work pattern emerged in my mind. Still not allowed to interrupt her, I paid close attention to what was important to her and listened to instructions she gave her design staff. I watched the way they worked with her, and also followed the usual communication and document snafus among departments. After a few weeks, I caught the drift of the normal workflow.

It was not routine for me to do this, and I had not worked in a business for almost ten years. Life completely changed from my early years in a communications manufacturing company where I held management positions. After I left, I had our second child, and then managed peach orchards for eight years before living in Thailand for a year. But some instinct for business systems kicked in and I ultimately proposed a management design for the interior design company, based on the standard principles and structure of a corporation. Once I improved the workflow, the tension evaporated. Since there was no avenue for advancement available to me, I realized that the modified infrastructure I had created could benefit other small businesses and I launched a service of my own.

Looking back over the years, I find that a vein of this kind of vibrancy was not uncommon in my life. Even though my eyes looked outward, often working against endless difficulties, that vein silently infused vigor into my heart and added energy to my movements. But I was totally unaware of this silent power inside until I lost it.

The years studying heart and spirit, and how these are connected to what we suppose is haphazard and serendipitous, have enabled me to perceive and recognize the regularity of instinctive power. There are characteristics of a system, a series of parts that *seem* to be unrelated but that are working together like gears of a clock. This is something we perceive more than understand. Once I caught the rhythm of my unconscious behavior and saw how the parts linked together, I saw a system wholly intuitive within my nature. I put my mind to work as a kind of mechanic to figure out *how* this system worked.

By following the trail of evidence left by my unconscious movements, there was a pattern; a sequence that repeated. Using my understanding of the scientific method—observe, hypothesize, test and correct—in a few years I had a theory that the life of the spirit has a rhythm, direction, and purpose. It has a life cycle.

Based on reasoning about how the human spirit "triumphs," I stepped out where there was no path before me. I became a scientist; an explorer. My intrepid heart took the lead and I followed where only my mind could go: I followed the trail with the eyes of my heart, and used my mind to work the evidence I collected.

Eleven: The Culture of the Self

We usually think of culture as a community of people who have developed characteristics that make the group recognizable. Culture is the same thing for one person. Each of us has certain characteristics that make us unique among billions of other people. By definition, *culture* is work that improves conditions. Each of us can improve our own condition by cultivating those things that help us improve and grow. The world unique to each person is her or his "self-culture."

We are recognized as groups by the variety of traits combined in unique ways. Different countries are characterized by habits held in common by the people: rituals, what they eat in common, how they speak. Within the United States there are different cultures. The South is distinct from the West and the Midwest is unlike New England. Culture forms in cities and towns and neighborhoods around unique traits.

Peering into the societal microscope, each family has a distinct culture, made up of unique individuals. So it is not far-fetched to say that each person has a distinct "self-culture," a world contained by the unique behavior and distinct preferences of the person.

What we do may appear the same as what others do, but the *way* we do things makes us distinct from others. As we mature and recognize what makes us unique we want to be known for the good qualities we have cultivated.

What a person does intuitively is based on a constant self-culture, inclinations and preferences built on a history of successes and failures. We work constantly to maintain our distinction from others wherever we go. This effort is unconscious; we *naturally* seek to improve the condition of our self-culture. Unconscious strategies are personal and intuitive, a natural desire for and efforts to increase good, for our own good.

Thought, ideas, and innovation have levels of maturation. Before we speak out our thoughts, things are rolling around in the back of our minds. For example, in any current situation there's the background to it and how we got to this point; how the personal interaction is going and how we might need to adjust to or work with the actions of others. There's timing to consider, and opportunity; health can be a factor, whether we have the energy now or not. When readiness and opportunity converge, we know it's time to speak or act.

We are easily moved by the forces of necessity and urgency outside of us but that is not the sum of life. If the will to live is not satisfied exactly, that slight dissatisfaction and its source will grow to become an urgency of a different kind. If we learn to be attentive to that quiet inner voice that speaks from the heart's mind, we can know about the good it seeks, how it is on the rise, and how it becomes ready to participate—for good.

In each day, we can progress toward satisfaction or become stuck in dissatisfaction. The more we delay giving respect to our heart's desire, the larger our dissatisfaction grows. If we impede the natural progress of good too long, unexpected events may disrupt the routine that seems safe, sending our careful plans into chaos. But genuine good is made clearer and stronger when the predictable fails.

In tragedy, loss, and death the value of human life takes on greater value. Priorities shift. We may realize that love was available to us but we didn't know it. A home can be a place of shelter or a domain of personal power. If we lose a home through fire or financial ruin, we may discover that family and friends care about us more than our props. So in great loss, love and good endure and good wins over all. In times of trouble we realize what is supremely important and become more willing to pay the price to have what is good.

As life cycles through good times and bad, we are changed inside. The changes inside cause us to mature—to recognize the difference between life as we want it to be, and life as it truly is. Maturity comes with the realization that we must know what life truly is, how life is made to encourage the continual expansion of good, and how the human quality of creativity is necessary to elevate *good* over progress. Because only in service to humanity is progress really valuable.

The Spirit of Creativity

Vision is seeing the value of a thing that does not yet exist and having some idea of how it can be made or built.

The arrangement of thoughts before action is different for every person, and conclusions that motivate action depend on this unique unspoken arrangement. This is actually the process of creativity. Creativity can lie dormant, or simply not be acknowledged, but it is worth investigating to find the ability to create that exists in every person. Ideas can change our existence.

The force of vibrant living is internal and is reflected in natural creativity; originality. Every day, individuals are changing the societal landscape in their corner of the world, in simple everyday contributions around their unique interests. At the root of subconscious thought and strategies is the *unconscious* will to live. The will to live is a force that makes us break free from conformity simply because we want to survive as unique individuals, to advance our own particular interests.

To break away from repetitive static living—even within our own self-culture—requires everyday passion, vision, and will. We are born to a purpose, and being unaware of that purpose can stifle the natural passion for life. Passion often forms around what is different from the usual and expected and is unique to the person. This preliminary cultivation occurs unconsciously.

We thrive around everyday creative people, and we enjoy what we all contribute to the conundrum that is life—in thought, voice, movement, and products of all kinds. To participate in everyday creativity only requires that we gradually reveal our differences, our oddities, and mature in them as we find our place in the world.

One artist applies her creative process as she responds to the unexpected in her day:

> "I start with my 'medium' for the day—my plan.
> But then something else gets thrown into the mix
> and I have to back off. Now I have to decide, which
> is the highest priority? Once I choose it, I can go
> ahead and move in it and then I'll *know* what
> comes next. In the flow, things come together and
> there's an extra dimension to it of loveliness and
> peace, truth and understanding. It's rich. If I had
> controlled it, that would not have happened."

The medium is what makes it possible to represent an idea, materially. The idea is much larger than the thing we're able to make. In being creative, we use whatever materials and resources available to us to make our idea a *thing*.

What is the mix of thought you put together so that the direction of your life is satisfying? Satisfaction can be in one small area where you feel progress on the path of passion or in small steps toward a unique high-level priority.

Where can your skills and talents be utilized toward a private good? Do you see a place where your initiative could make a difference—in your occupation, in your family or in a significant relationship? Or is it in something that has no definite presence yet, something that teases your mind and draws you to imagine it?

Twelve: A New Way of Working

We can be happy in work when we are competent, challenged, creative, appreciated, and growing. Having all these things at once is the goal of life, and we direct our lives through work. The pay does not always have to be in dollars. What we do unconsciously is fluid, immediate, and is a demonstration of natural ability.

What we do from the heart is who we are to the world. If we bring heart into all we do, we are competent and satisfied, first, and then the surface things are also more satisfying. We are available for love in all that we do, because we are moving in what we love. Each of us is designed to live and thrive naturally from the inside toward the outside, from our deepest knowledge, through our hearts and will, caring to bring who we are to the surface beyond our own skin. It all starts with the burning in our hearts. If we don't know what that is, or if we deny it a place in our lives, all that's left is rote and role, function and utility. Many people are highly motivated by money, above all else. If you are still reading this, you're probably not one of them; you're one of us. When your heart is in what you do, you are renewed by work, not depleted, and money is merely utilitarian.

I struggled with the idea of adequate compensation for the work I do. As the economy moves and changes, it's always hard to pin that down. As a consultant, I had to determine what is the value of my time and whether my contribution improved the personal productivity of my client. In some cases, it had to be a *feeling* of adequate compensation, on my side; on the client's side it was a feeling of having been helped, that my work made a difference.

Now that governments and businesses are shifting to a new global economy, our sensitivity at the personal level is heightened. Workers have taken hold of the tools of technology, and the pressure is on to use them to create. This is a change in the occupational landscape, similar to the time when workers moved from farming to industrial work in the cities. But now we have the opportunity to create new goods and services, create new professions, and start businesses of our own. It's a revolution of personal fulfillment but there is not an economy firmly attached to it, yet. We must take steps to help shape the future and use our natural senses—our intuition—to balance the economic factors.

National and corporate income levels do not pertain to the creative solo entrepreneur. We have to start where we have information about the dollar value of our skills in the marketplace and adjust it locally and personally. When you have a unique offering there is still an arena where that good or service is recognized, but we are doing the work ourselves, directly, feeling our way forward. It's a bit primitive compared to high finance and business tradition, but it's the economics of new growth in society, exciting and vibrant. We can feel it.

By working closely from the heart we keep that vibrant living force that moves us to work and to create, rather than to look for a place already prepared for us. Creating a new economy takes participation at all levels of society, and at the turn of the century the burden falls on individuals more than ever before.

The challenge is to recover the natural person that was lost in the era of information technology. Companies do not create; people create. As we keep more of our ideas for ourselves, we encompass the natural mechanisms of business development. The "solopreneur" becomes designer, manufacturer, sales, and bookkeeper for the enterprise.

Thanks to The Great Recession of 2008 and the economic crisis that followed, we are forced to use our wits and free time rather than money. We work from home offices because it is more cost effective, and raise our status as we raise our heads.

A World Unique

Each person's life is a world unique to herself or himself, a mass of information that begins collecting at birth. We move from an original impression on us and begin building a singular perspective, with automatic responses to experiences in an environment that is already in motion. We begin to form opinions internally, based on how we are affected, choosing a way that makes sense to us. We work out private priorities, and they shift and change as we mature and share life with others. We develop a thirst for acceptance, agreement, and most of all, for love.

This world of "me" is largely unconscious, unspoken. And yet it's easy to intuit that this private world is right because the way we assemble details is unique and always makes sense to "me."

We find out how to succeed in making small, gradual gains for what's most important to us, working around where life relentlessly opposes our will. We learn how life *is*, as opposed to what we want it to be. Wisdom and knowledge come from the mistakes, failures, and losses in finding what works, and also where life will never give us our way.

Not only do *we* have a heart, *life* also has a heartbeat—a regular pulse that maintains its own singular, global priorities. It supports people as creatures of life, just as it sustains plants and animals. If we understand our own nature, it's easier to see how life sustains human life *according* to our nature. *Life* supports life, and our way of living draws from life what we need to make our lives happier and healthier. This is what it takes for humanity to survive.

If a living thing is not protected and nurtured where its life is sustained, it will begin to die. People are not happy with a marginal existence. We want to thrive, within. No matter what our circumstances, it is in our very nature to find a way to secure the survival of identity, and identity lives in the heart, sustaining the human spirit.

Work as Personal Flow

Work can be an outgrowth of what we love to do. And what we love to do, we do effortlessly and happily. Begin to recognize what you do effortlessly and happily and you'll find what you love to do. It's unconscious.

Being in a personal flow happens when we own our time, protect where we are different, and value contributions that make a difference even if not recognized or appreciated.

Work is not necessarily a job. It is the exertion we expend to accomplish an objective. When we see our natural gifts at work, it feels good. Feeling good at work energizes us and we actually want to do more "work." Happiness is not in what you do as much as it is in the way you do things. When we can do things our way, we have a sense of value, first, and then a sense of power. We have come to an era in history when doing our own thing is appreciated as a service or as enhancing the quality of life, rather than as selfishness or self-centeredness. In order to give, we have to know what we've got.

The true engine of good is in the heart, in the heart's *mind*—in its will, its intention, and its strategy. The heart's mind appears in 20/20 hindsight. We can see the good that has happened, beyond our intent and work. We can also see where it was less than good, and how it *could have been* good if only we had done this or that differently. Hindsight is very informative, and the longer the timeframe, the clearer the picture.

To do what we do well, we need to be happy in work. It doesn't matter what you do for work. Work occupies our time and can give us value, but it can also make us feel unimportant. Being happy in work is not based on how much money you make or whether you feel important. Being happy in work is a combination of several things: natural talents; a place to serve with those talents; response, recognition and/or appreciation from those we serve; getting past survival toward flourishing in life.

We chisel our lives out daily, trying to have it all. And there is more than just work. Our relationships form the undercurrent that makes life easier, more difficult, happy or somber. We are happier if we are able to show up as the same person, from the heart; the same person who is at work or at rest, in the formalities of a profession or relaxed and at play.

Being true to ourselves, knowing what's appropriate for the time and place, while flexing with circumstances and making room for relationships to grow—this is something we are built to do, naturally. But we live in a world of institutions, businesses, banks, and governmental regulation that often override human connection. Human connection must begin with being in touch with our own humanity as individuals.

Having wholeness as a person brings happiness to all that we do. Being whole is not something you do or a way to learn. Being whole is the hardest work we do as human beings. Being whole is showing up as yourself, knowing that you bring all you are and all you know into life as it presents itself.

When we understand how the heart works without our direct attention, we find in the heart the place of our highest competence and our greatest satisfaction. They are one and the same.

Working Unconsciously Well

The work of both artists and entrepreneurs is contained in personal vision: We see in our mind's eye something that does not yet exist and we must wrestle time and matter until the vision emerges as reality. Ideas may come frequently, and some of us have new ideas all the time. But the real proof of meaning in work, whether creating art or business, comes out of the natural cooperation of life forces. *We are life forces that can cooperate with all the other life forces.*

I found a sequence in my unconscious responses when caught off-guard. There was something at work in my own mind that required no conscious effort. All my years of survival by effort and paranoia had nothing whatsoever to contribute. Over time, I gradually shifted away from natural inclination and personal preference toward the new, unconsciously good motivation. Rather than a self-serving personal choice, I found that living true from the heart automatically factored in respect for others and was both fruitful and satisfying.

Heart, in the end, is primarily relationship-based. Since I cannot know the heart goals of others and where they might be in that pursuit, I learned to restrain an all-out myopic self-interest. Fear could have kept me from allowing the machinery of my life to rebalance itself. But I had abandoned fear as a motivator in favor of this newfound source of positive natural energy.

Here are the elements of working a life process in the creativity age:

- Freedom to create, solving problems to move in the heart's direction.

- Tools for creating and moving in society: computers and the Internet.
- Business-as-service principles, inviolable as the basis of earning a living.
- Self-discipline to make progress on heart-driven goals.
- Originality and creative freedom, tools, entrepreneurship, ownership.

Originality: "Be yourself" is the very definition of distinction. Exhilaration in the leadership of the heart is a satisfying pursuit that is not diminished by working alone and is undaunted by the lack of money. The natural heart's mind was running in concert with the nature of life, and this intangible nature supported my intangible heart; they were in sync.

Where my heart had failed me before in times of stress and tragedy, now it was renewed and grew stronger at each level of purging in the fires. It was the passing of time and life, in all its trials and obstructions, but with a rhythm that brought harmony between the outside world and me.

Freedom to Create

Over and over we find that attaining the reality of a dream is not satisfying in itself. So we find new projects as one thing attained opens our eyes to what more can be done. I found that my dream got bigger and easier. Why is that? Because life would hand me what I needed to fulfill my purpose and I was ready to receive it.

I came to discover my contribution and my purpose by following my heart's mind.

However, life is such that even though my dream gets continually bigger and easier, my understanding of my purpose is never complete. I keep moving ever onward spurred by the joy and satisfaction infused into every day. The ideal is almost never attained, but the pursuit of an ideal—including one's ideal self-image—is how life moves forward in a positive direction. Though it took many long years, I eventually woke up to the fact that freedom and responsibility are equal partners. And if I were to exercise freedom responsibly, I must respect the right of others to exercise freedom according to their convictions.

The nature of life is that it is never perfect and never will be. Therefore, to accept imperfection is critical to being realistic about what is attained in a lifetime. The personal happiness I experience every day is in knowing that, in the pursuit, I constantly make gains toward my ideal.

Perspective: All of Us

We can generally agree on ideals such as love, compassion, cooperation, freedom, and equality. But in carrying out our respective pursuits, the details appear differently. The heart of life itself is good. It has no particular interest in any one person's goals; everyone gets life equally, according to its arbitrary whims. But life's nature only seems haphazard because we make plans according to human nature and human thinking.

Unconscious action is the opposite of planned action, but it is by no means mindless. Human nature also consists of spirit. When we factor in this fourth trait with the experiences of the intellectual, emotional, and the physical there will be more truth in our perspective.

There's a whole spectrum of ability and willingness to work, from working under compulsion to working for someone to reach your own goals, to working for the sake of working because that is what stands between you and your dream. This is the unconscious vein of motivation.

Personal vision inspires work, creativity, authority, and ownership. The information age is the past, having provided tools for new goods and services. The future will be what individuals make of it.

Thirteen: Bringing Heart to Life and Work

A whole-hearted engagement with work springs out of the lives we live. The art of perspective is to work from a place of total ownership, holding on to our hearts: owning our time, our productivity, minding our own business, creating personal professional standards, and sometimes creating unique professions. We can be flexible with life as an extension of ourselves, and manage finances as we manage ourselves. We can allow for time and the cycles of life to support us as we work out a unique freedom.

Use these four steps to check your connection with life and work, from inside, out:

- Start with Heart
- Free your mind
- Watch for fruit
- Enjoy the process

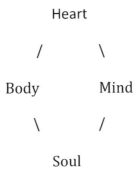

Start with Heart

The heart gently urges us in an easy, unconscious tendency toward good. Only you can detect the urgency in your heart and follow it. Use the ideas expressed in this book to recognize where your heart wants to go. In my stories, identify similarities and differences between your mind and mine. By checking your inner sense of agreement and disagreement, you can become better at knowing yourself—who you are—in the deepest level of awareness.

Free the Mind

This is a critical exercise. If all our decisions and plans are based on what is possible with our available material resources, we can become very discouraged. If what we dream takes more than we can imagine having, we may put all our efforts into acquiring more.

But people who have gained all the material wealth they wanted are notoriously still not satisfied. We will always want more than we have. But that's a good thing. It's the constant unconscious desire to improve our circumstances that motivates us to put effort into changing those circumstances.

The "Free your Mind" exercise acknowledges that it's a good thing to imagine the best circumstances for our lives. But in this strategy that desire must come from the heart.

Let your mind roam from your heart, looking toward all that you hope for in life. Ask yourself, *If my world were to be exactly the way I would enjoy it, giving me the greatest satisfaction, what would it look like?* By freeing your mind, you will be able to recognize help toward that end, if it comes along.

Watch for Fruit

Here's where life gets interesting. Having done the hard part, freeing your mind from the limitations you see in the world around you, when something crosses your path—and in some cases, is virtually handed to you—that is a piece of what it takes to reach your ideal, you'll naturally take hold of it.

The heart is nourished and alive when you value its place and give it space to grow. The matchup between heart and hand, through allowing life to choose the right time, sends a thrill through the heart and mind. Sensations of joy are expressed, body and soul.

Enjoy the Process

The convergence of heart, soul, mind and body in working out the ideal self, is still subject to the *nature* of life. Nothing changes that. "Enjoy the Process" means that, when you are at work, and the challenges are real, remember that you are where you set your heart to be.

It's the way it is in climbing a mountain. From the valley, and at a distance, the mountain is beautiful and majestic. We want to be there, in that high place. So we set out to climb the mountain. The closer we get, the more our view of the mountain peak is obscured. As we move up the mountain and get deeper into the climb, we don't see the peak at all. We see dirt, rocks, trees... in other words, there's nothing special in the appearance or in the experience.

We draw from the knowledge that we are in the process of realizing our dream. We are moving to that mountain peak, regardless of what we see; regardless of the ordinary work of walking and climbing. We are heartened—we *enjoy the process*—because we are where our hearts led us to be.

The Road from Inspiration to Reality

An idea inspired in the heart always benefits a person, and it usually inspires others in some way even before it proves itself.

This is what brings hope. Hope exists in the absence of the thing we desire. Once we have it, hope is fulfilled. So having a vision is hope that fuels the work required to fulfill the vision.

An engineer or designer begins with an idea that solves a problem, physical, intellectual, or emotional. Then the intangible perfection of design meets the tangible and imperfect means needed to make the design a reality. A designer can only hold to the perfect vision while the materials (reality) yield to the pressure. The designer must accommodate or overcome the obstacles. The substance of the design can change, but the vision persists.

Attainment of the vision is a product of the designer's (owner's) ability to accept the real place of the vision as a thing of service to others. Working the idea works *us*! What is happening inside us as designers/owners when the design must be modified? The process of hurling ourselves against obstacles results in some successes and some failures. Through a life process of trial and error, modification and persistence, we learn what can be changed—and what changes us.

The idea may broaden and develop differently from what we imagined. This is the same way we mature as distinct persons. What we are, in the first moments of our birth, remains constant and matures over time. Our concept of life and what is possible and available to us may change, but hearts don't change or age.

We retain a unique outlook from within, even as we age, as our appearance changes, and as circumstances shift over our lifetime. The heart's mind is set, carrying out its function throughout our life.

Fourteen: Self-Renewing Motivation

A Compass for the Whole Self

We know intuitively that perfect good exists. Like the North Star, perfect good is a reference point that exists outside of time, reminding us of a world beyond the physical, intellectual and emotional experience.

Our lives revolve around the unstoppable, self-renewing life force in the human design. It is the chlorophyll to our growth, the sap to our tree, the desire to overcome, against all physical evidence to the contrary. It is the human spirit. It holds the wisdom of living and gives meaning to our lives.

Doing my own thing successfully depends upon me being accountable to myself for my heart's high goals. When we create high standards for our own performance, we can create unique professions even if they fit under familiar labels like "consultant," "engineer," "designer," "sales," or "marketing."

View life as a natural process that we are made to live out. In the natural human hierarchy, the spirit is the living force that gives us breath, life and movement. The spirit enlivens the intellect, emotion, and renews physical energy.

At our core, we are spiritual beings in a flesh-and-blood body. We move in intuitive "paths" that have direction and reasonable order. We each *unconsciously* do exactly what we want to do, stirred by a particularly human instinct that seeks meaning and purpose more than physical comfort and material success. If there is a human instinct, it is moving us beyond mere survival to where we <u>strive to thrive</u>.

We cannot put our finger on what *spirit* is, exactly, but we can observe its movements, like the wind. The *spirit* of a thing is its righteous intention, above and beyond an action or series of decisions. *Spirit* is life and breath in motion. So the effect of spirit can be seen in what we say we do *unconsciously*, what is automatic and intuitive, without intention of forethought.

When we move with the spirit of living energy, the mind serves as strategist, the soul as the will and expression of energy, and the body as the observable force through activity. Because individuality is the source of innovation and creativity, we must draw on the human spirit that "triumphs" over fear and doubt when circumstances demand courage and vision.

If we judge by what we experience externally, goodness seems to happen accidentally. By attaching our minds, bodies and emotions to the greater power, the spirit, we see with *our heart's eye* the place where goodness exists in its own continuity. The *heart's mind* is constantly and effortlessly at work *for* us, taking us toward our heart's desire.

Fifteen: The Rise of the Human Spirit

Astonishing transformation is natural and normal.

The human spirit is intangible, and its influence comes as a breath to the heart and in whispers to the mind. Life is designed to revive and renew, whether in our ecosystem, in each species of plants and animals, or in the particularly astonishing way that the human spirit revives and renews body, mind, and emotion. We naturally and automatically reach for something better.

Eruptions from the heart can capsize the boat of intention in which we've been sailing toward our own ideas or in the strength of our own resolve. The spirit rises often *because* of the tragedies we live through; we're forced to stop and re-evaluate how we live. The need in our hearts rises up, searching for a reality greater than what life appears to be.

In our natural experience we look out through our eyes and feel impacts on body and soul. But as spirit-beings, our deepest unconscious knowledge about good is in the uniqueness of human nature. It is revealed in the world *behind* our eyes and how we create our individual perspectives. We follow what motivates us emotionally, intellectually and physically; the tendency is natural, automatic, and unconscious. The heart acts as a place where the intangible spirit and the senses-oriented soul converge and make us unique.

Spirit is increasingly relevant in our lives. In this discussion about the heart's mind and our unconscious certainty of good we look to the *nature* of spirit, not to our beliefs about spirit*ual* things. When we know our own hearts we gain a nonreligious understanding of the nature of spirit. We can discover the source of original thought, where spirit moves upon the heart and informs the heart's mind. The demand of the times is for exceptional personal performance and we are searching within ourselves to meet that demand.

An unconscious desire to live and grow—triggers an automatic renewal of spirit. In experiencing spontaneous renewal I found evidence of the "me" that I am: what I am that no one else is or can be. The real me lived in my spirit, knew its destination and never veered off course. I found this system to be reliable and predictable in its method of working underneath the surface, and it did not alter course, no matter what happened on "the topside." Gradually, as I put all my attention on my heart's mind, I find a place of peace behind it. I become positive and willing, intellectually; calm and accepting, emotionally; and ready for appropriate action physically. I become invigorated and inspired, and curious about the world of the distinct "self" in others.

Choose to live close to the heart. It ensures that what we say and do has the liveliness of growth rather than weariness of endurance. We can see how life supports each of us in doing what is put in our hands to do, to be what we are born to be. As we exercise intuitive ability, leadership is subtle and natural and we become willing to take risks to satisfy our true heart's intention. Taking risk appropriately restores the private thrill of adventure and zest for life. And in the process, we discover our natural capacity to form heartfelt relationships of every kind.

Sixteen: Making the Unfamiliar Familiar

The process of something unfamiliar becoming familiar is completely automatic. Even when we enjoy some benefit in our lives, once it is a regular occurrence, it falls to the background. People can adjust to anything: poverty or riches; happiness or depression.

Life proves its ultimate power over everyone, even the very wealthy, the very successful, the loved, and the happy. At some point, those people also experience poverty of some kind, defeat at some time, rejection by someone, and some sadness. "Into everyone's life a little rain must fall." These sayings offer comfort in the fact that no one is exempt. All suffer as I do. That is the human condition. If we base our acceptance on circumstances as if we cannot change them, we naturally feel defeated. That's because change is a condition humans prefer. The prospect of overcoming and dominating is encouraging because the norm of life is that there is so much we cannot control. Humans may be the dominant life form but we are subject to nature, same as any creature.

The human condition also contains an ability to access a higher power connected to the eternal and transcendent, the inherent quality of being human: the quality of *spirit*. When we have spirit, no force on Earth can keep us down. Even if we fall, we will rise again. Spirit is different within each person. It is the power to transform mere facts and reality into possibility and the hope of new conquests. Imagination is the power to see what isn't there—yet.

Change introduces the possibility of new territory to be had, something as yet unknown to a person. The union of heart and soul transforms unfamiliar territory into kingdoms to be had. Unconsciously, the heart overrides fact and reality. The unconscious response to the confrontation that change presents releases the mind from conscious logic; relieves the mind of "facing reality" to follow with mind and body the more certain *intuitive* knowledge.

Change gives us the opportunity for conflict, the chance to assert our "right" against life. We reject the assumption that we are subject to life, that we are dominated by it. If we are not subject to life, and instead can gain a sense of power over it, it is solely a private internal victory. No one wins in life 100% of the time; our private victories are important only to ourselves. We balance the "figures" on our side. We "figure in" assumptions where facts are unknown, and our assumptions lean in toward a favorable outcome. These private victories make all the difference to our confidence, and we go further on our private mission.

The theory proposed here is that the natural human mechanism of spirit transforms a heart *concept* into a *fact* of good. It begins with capturing change and subjecting it to the private world of the spirit's owner as the higher power. Only a power higher than the physical can overcome adversity. Only a power greater than human power can overcome the physical, and establish the ultimate goal of good.

We know there will always be change, and yet when it comes, it is often unexpected. The surprise we feel in the face of change indicates a norm, that what we expect usually happens. So, unconsciously we know that the majority of life can be anticipated. We react to the impact of something unexpected, but we overcome the shock. Life surrounds the change with its regularity, and the change is no longer change; it becomes familiar.

Seventeen: Finding the "me"

Keeping true to one's natural self enhances our ability to give out of what we love, and from the gifts inherent in our nature. Rather than self-discovery in physical, intellectual or emotional abilities, this will be a look into the functions and competencies at work in the heart. We must see the heart's mind and know how it works independent of the intellect. We must give it our attention, understand it, and include it as a function of our whole being.

Being introspective as a writer I was already familiar with my internal landscape, so I dug deeper inward to find what lay behind the thinking that seemed so rational and yet failed so completely. I found a logic that worked without my intention: the heart's mind. Incredibly, I got answers that were even more profound than the questions, custom fit answers that satisfy me.

In the absence of heart motivation, and in the overwhelming dominance of rote and necessity, the random appearance of energy electrified me. At first, these appeared in flashes and I couldn't tell where they came from. I just felt an effect. But it wasn't long before I collected information, characteristics that were so unusual, but pieced together the pieces began to make sense. Here was a thing within me that I never knew was there.

I separated out the traits I recognized, the natural "human as creature" and its logic, and then looked to see what was left. The comparison led to more questions:

- What is behind the things we do that are unplanned and purely unique to one's unspoken, pre-conscious instinct?

- What is that nature of humanity, the design that makes each person unique?

- Why does life continue on, dragging me with it, despite my deadness and lack of hope?

My curiosity was an unspoken, preconscious instinct, and when I pointed my attention toward the questions, I was energized. My mind became active and occupied, lying in wait for the appearance of this elusive energy that surged unexpectedly. I got better at recognizing the impulses that came through me, out of nowhere, and wrote down my observations quickly when I realized what happened. I began to capture impulsive statements I made without thinking and to trace them back to what provoked my outbursts.

These were nothing but pieces, like faint marks on a trail. Not until I looked back did the pieces link into a form and a direction, like fingerprints made visible with a powder, revealing what their owner had touched. By observing over long stretches of time, and laboring to find words to adequately express what I saw, the habits of my other self took on a pattern. There was repetition; and finally, variation, nuance and rhythm, like the workings of a clock.

Now, twenty years later, I have terminology to describe this natural phenomenon, a system that bridges spirit and soul in the heart, and connects heart with mind and body. I call it "the heart's mind" because the way it moves through time is methodical, sequential, autonomous, and unstoppable. The heart's mind appears in a person's unconscious responses that show her or his natural inclination and nature, but on the surface, unconscious responses can seem haphazard and serendipitous. Since we judge what we see with reasoning based on what we see and hear, the silent path of unconscious intention is invisible to the reality-bound intellect.

Innate Knowledge

So much of life is about what happens outside of our bodies that we can forget that there's a lot going on inside. What goes on inside doesn't always show up on the outside—not obviously, anyway.

There are moments when we're caught off-guard and we say or do things impulsively; it's unconscious. Those impulses tell us more about ourselves than what we plan or figure out in our minds because they come from knowledge greater than our worldly experience. It is a *knowing* that doesn't occur to us to explain, and couldn't if we tried, because it is a truth built into us our whole lives.

Our particular blend of will and emotion makes us unique, makes up the *soul*, and our unconscious response to change is evidence of the soul. *Will* is a strong desire or passion that comes from heart and soul. It's "where there's a will, there's a way," despite obstacles. Desire and passion fuel the journey we take to satisfy our souls—to have heart and soul.

We can work from this unique place—where will and emotion fuse together into passion—and find a way for the vision to be expressed and made manifest. When the unique passion that we feel is expressed, we have an impact on the world around us, an impact on the hearts of others. That impact can be positive (building up) or negative (tearing down). Either way, inside we feel confident that what we are doing is right because we're doing right by ourselves.

I'm doing right by my heart as I write this. I am compelled; I cannot do otherwise. This is my passion. I am strong-willed, as far as these ideas go. I own them because they are unique to me. I am being myself when I boldly express how I am different from other people. Words and actions that burst from my heart impulsively are unconscious and true. No matter if I retract or embrace what I unconsciously reveal, it is my true heart's mind.

You Already Know This

As I describe the way I am inside, I hope you will see that you are a certain way inside, too, that you are either like me or unlike me, or some variation in between.

Do you struggle with being understood, as you believe you are inside? Do you often give the "wrong impression" when you talk about your passion? Do others treat you differently, different from what you think they should know and respect about you?

If you answer "Yes" to any of the questions, you are like me inside.

When I describe what I experience inside, and you know the same thing inside, it proves that we are both human. Being human is the inner experiences we share, as well as the outer experiences.

To know and understand your own heart's mind can help you know your heartfelt place in the world, the place you can own, inside>out. Moving outward from the heart transforms all that you do. The effort is in staying close to the heart and returning to heart when we drift.

Eighteen: "spirit" is Human

A friend once asked me, "What is the *human* spirit?" She asked it because, as a religious person, conversations about *spirit* tend to center on God and the *Holy* Spirit. She picked up on my reference to *spirit* that was not religious.

We know all about the human spirit, and yet I, too, had not thought of my spirit in terms other than as "spirituality." My deep search for a reliable inner compass led me to discover the *nature* of the spirit—how it behaves.

Spirit is intangible and incomprehensible to the conscious mind. Starting with the sign of natural life—the real electric spark that told me *I am alive!*—I traced those rare occasions back to their origin within myself. This was introspection of a magnitude I had never experienced before.

I worked backward from the spark and where it showed up in spontaneous words or actions. Since every other kind of word or action was a labor of dragging my body around, doing necessary things by rote, these words and actions had force and power enough to trigger a dynamic in me, from head to toe.

At first, these occasions were months apart. But as I learned to recognize the kind of sensation it was, I was on it like a hound dog. After a few years of this, no conditioned "dead" response could hold my attention like this living force.

The nature of spirit is that we cannot see or know it, but I was able to perceive the very subtle evidence of *spirit* in how it shows up. Like the effect of wind, I followed the visible signs of the impulses of my heart. Those impulses came unbidden by conscious intention.

Evidence of spirit/heart is easier to detect than *spirit*, itself. Unplanned, immediate action and impulsive words spoken with passion come straight from the heart. We sometimes cannot contain our passion and truth blurts out, whether we want it or not. A situation can so stir the heart that we spring to action, not thinking about the consequences.

I picked up on cues in language that further enlightened me about *spirit*. I noticed simple references to *spirit* in everyday conversation. I also noticed how these were completely unrelated to *spirit* in the religious sense.

We use stimuli to explain *spirit*. "Triumph of the human spirit," "team spirit," "kindred spirits," "with you in spirit," "a free spirit," and "the spirit of the law" are all nonreligious expressions of spirit. We intuitively know what we mean, and to define these phrases actually takes the life out of them.

Spirit and heart behave similarly: "I had my heart set on (something) ," "wears her heart on her sleeve," "have a heart," "working wholeheartedly"—these are as common in language as "team spirit" and "kindred spirits." A "broken heart" seems very much like a "broken spirit" and "in my heart of hearts" could mean deep in my spirit.

With All My Heart

It is impossible to care about work if the heart/spirit is broken. I worked, but only by habit, and only out of necessity: to feed, clothe, and shelter my body. In the desolation of heart, I could barely see the point of working *solely* to feed, clothe, and shelter my body. Some might say I was depressed, but since I was working on a solution with hope it was not depression. It was an acknowledgment of fact; a fact I intended to change.

Because there is a God, and because I believe the world is a thing created by God—and because I believe that God is perfect good, with the only perfect understanding of love—I believed there had to be evidence of God in the world, intrinsic to the situation in which the human creature was placed. My certainty led me to search for evidence of a *natural* connection between the "me," as creature, and the total situation around me, from stars to earth; from spirit to Spirit.

I concluded that the *nature* of nature is to provide for and support human life and our need for nurture. The difference is that *functional* life is insufficient for humans; we need purpose and meaning for human life to endure till the end of time. So my question became, how does life support the *spirit* of humankind, the vital force for its growth and success?

I was old enough to have fulfilled nearly every major endeavor *functional* life offered. I had married, raised children, worked in a way that was satisfying, and was seeing the start of the next generation of families from me. I had recovered from poor health. I had, to that point, had a vibrant spiritual life that gave me joy and strength for adversity. I had become self-educated and responsible enough to provide leadership to people around me.

In the end, all of that resourcefulness was burned up in the effort to survive the destruction of the life I had built with my own wits. I could lead no one, including myself. Physical survival meant that I must work to feed the body, merely to live on. But here was the problem: I had run out of the *heart* to sustain the *practical* demands of survival. So when I did exhibit motivation, it was an anomaly.

When I found myself active in the midst of something I did not consciously choose, I traced back through to find what led me there. I had skipped intellectual judgment and responded intuitively because my *heart* was touched. The spontaneous responses and movement were powerful—and effortless! I would then think backwards to what I saw, heard, and thought—what led to unconsciously spoken words or an unconscious course of action. In those cases, my reaction was instant and straight from the heart.

Hmmm...

Putting my attention to unraveling this puzzle was work of a different sort. It was *big*—and easy for me. Through years of this privately motivated task, I can now make a connection between what I enjoy doing and activity that touches my heart. I am closer to seeing that love is the most powerful motivator of all.

Let Go and Catch the Drift

I am a boat on the ocean. I am caught in an ocean stream and it carries me in its way. I move but exert no effort. The scenery approaches and rolls past me; the horizon approaches. I accept what I see because I am at rest in the protection of my boat.

I am a raft on a river, caught in its flow; sometimes it is still and peaceful; sometimes I hit white water rapids. Unlike real-life rafting, I am in no danger as long as I stay in the raft.

I am an explorer, having no preconceived idea of what I will find. Every turn on the way astonishes me. I have never seen such sights before. Thrilling!

The good hit me like a freight train quite unexpectedly. Having tasted the good, I see that it is worth the price it extracted from me. Now I am a person open to the good. Knowing the cost, I accept the cost.

Unexpected good:

- Protection for my heart, mind, body and soul when I had no strength to cover myself.
- Joining of family hearts in true love, forged by adversity.
- An end of domestic abuse.
- Release of undiscovered natural abilities.
- True spiritual understanding, free of dogma.
- Restoration of relationships in honesty.

When we can see that the flow of life sustains and provides for all life on the planet, including the human spirit that lives in the body, there is integration, wholeness, and a perception of the gestalt beyond the fragments we experience. The natural gravitation of the physical is downward; entropy and decay. The natural pull of the spirit defies gravity; it rises as the material is consumed. Life is continually renewed in the process. This applies to the human spirit as much as to the life force of all living things: our bodies and for plants and animals. Who cares for the birds? Who cares for us? The world is designed to provide, not for the exclusive benefit of any one being but for the whole earthly network that works together as a whole.

In observing the flow of life through my heart, at one point what was filling me up inside began to flow beyond me. Just after a breakthrough, the effort I continued to apply was suddenly ineffective. The more I exerted my will to go further in the direction of some project success the tighter the unseen constraints seemed, frustrating my every attempt.

In this bound and powerless state, I could only watch with my heart's eye. Where I had thought the success of a project or a situation was because of and the reason for my personal breakthrough, suddenly I was not in the picture. The work I had begun continued but now it moved forward without me. Fixed in this position and restrained from acting I learned the truth. Some *thing* in life had allowed me to participate in *its* larger purpose. Being left out of my "important" work I could see what was happening around and beyond myself. I was humbled by the unexpected good that came without my effort. Life itself had nurtured me and others around me, using the work as a vehicle.

The concept of material progress happening without our direct effort is very unappealing. We think that, if any good happens, it is because *we* intend it, that we *make* it happen. But through this observation I came to understand how nature works as an undercurrent bringing us closer to general improvement. The nature of life makes our effort a contribution to history, *while* we work on the conscious level.

Flow is a natural phenomenon. It is a current running underneath life, uniting people, places, and things in events. Internally, it is a place of harmony between ourselves and what we do. *Flow* is cooperation between spirit and matter, where our hands work directly from the vision in our hearts. We perceive the flow; sometimes we catch the flow, go with the flow, or move against the flow.

There is a wonderful analogy for the union of heart and matter in the way that ships move in the "paths" in the sea. In the early history of navigation, when ships crossed the ocean, navigators struggled against tides and currents sometimes finding that the ocean changed their course.

When the ocean currents were discovered, virtual conveyor belts were revealed going in various directions through the waters. The navigators plotted a course so that the ship took the "path" heading in the desired direction. Not only did they get to the desired destination, they traveled faster with less effort.

The ship can represent the body, and the navigator the heart within. The currents are the flow of life that can seem serendipitous (unexpected good) or haphazard (things that "don't make sense," to our way of thinking).

We can track our movement like boats on the currents, the waves, and the storms of life. We can't tell what moves life, but like the ocean currents we can see an effect. Inside the "ship," the spirit moves about freely without managing the things of the body. Where flow can seem serendipitous and haphazard, there is a way to track our position in and against the flow.

Stress

When private inner stress builds up from denying the heart's mind and we suppress the good with an artificial front that gets approval, we tire from holding up the front that is far from our hearts. Eventually the inner dissonance weakens will, mind, and/or body. If we let it, the heart can lead us to solid ground again, showing us what's most important in life: our desire to live and what it takes to have that desire.

Working without heart, without personal satisfaction, is draining. Working *with* heart, from personal strengths and natural gifts, can transform the very fiber of daily life. Through what we lose on the surface the heart teaches us what really matters, in the heart where the vigor of life resides and transcends difficulty.

Being heart-driven is not being selfish; rather, it plays a part in delivering the highest good for all concerned in the end. The concert of harmonious intentions begins with agreement within ourselves, among heart, soul, mind, and body: from a spirit that renews the intellect and is expressed in emotion and action.

The human spirit is a compass connected with a greater true purpose, and it rouses the heart's deep response. Our hearts feel the call to "true north," are happy when we're on course, and become uneasy if we veer off course. If we stray too far from the heart's mind, the intellect, emotions, and body (health) become uneasy too, which can lead to dis-ease.

In 1994, at my dad's funeral, I realized there were sharp pains radiating through my right hand. I shook it and rubbed it, but nothing alleviated the pain for more than a few minutes. I ignored it, of course. Since there was no apparent cause, I thought it would just go away. I got used to it but after several months the pain started creeping up my arm. Eventually it flourished at my elbow in excruciating pain. I began using my left hand more to give it some relief. After a while my left arm began to manifest the same sharp, electric pain.

When I couldn't alter the pain in my arms, I had to trim my activities. I stopped volunteering, and my absence eventually kept the phone from ringing. Even at home I was down to a bare minimum, doing only the unavoidable and necessary things. I called on our then ten-year-old son to lift things for me. Over a period of about two years he was patient, but there were days when he and I were so frustrated we began to think it would never end. I looked for help from doctors and chiropractors but no one found the cause, and nothing brought relief.

Finally, I overcame the despair of having no solution, and confronted my distracted husband until he faced the problem with me. We knew a young chiropractor who had a reputation among our friends for his unconventional approach. He was the butt of snide remarks and jokes, but we decided to give him a shot. In one session of cranial manipulation, he stopped the electric nerve pain. I could feel there was still damage, but there was no new pain. It took months of rest and care before my arms healed, and it took years to fully recover strength in my arms.

I tell this story because the cause was stress—emotional stress that affected me, mind and body. But even in the depths of pain and frustration, something rose up in me and compelled me to write. It was very painful, and I worked slowly tapping at the keyboard with one finger. But at that time, I felt that if I didn't write I would die. Writing became a lifeboat that helped me survive the crisis, and I learned what meets *my* need for survival; it was no one's need but mine.

Looking back on that time and how writing has always been at the core of my life, I know writing is how I am sustained—heart, soul, mind and body. My search for happiness is neither the road heavily traveled, nor the road less traveled. The path of happiness is walking the road no one knows to travel but me.

New Definitions for Living With Spirit

Heart: The deepest essence of your being; the root of your personality.

Soul: Where will and emotion converge into motivation.

Mind: The place where decisions are made, giving direction to your life.

Body: The vehicle for all action, and that which facilitates or restricts ability.

Priority: The hierarchy of importance where we place people, situations, things and ideas in relation to one another.

Unconscious: The part of being that is before conscious or subconscious thought. It is the intuitive knowledge that is the human, a living navigation system that guides us from birth to death.

Unconscious Good: The positive quality of the human spirit that makes all people inclined to improve their situation. It is the impulse of human nature that is spiritual, involuntary, knowing, and of love's essence. It is the life force that draws us toward a good, just as a plant is drawn to sunlight.

Work (not to be confused with "job"): Motion of the body with intention. Work is the natural imperative of desire, the activity necessary to realize and manifest ideas.

Perfect Good: The unattainable for which we, nevertheless, strive to reach daily. It is the source of dissatisfaction with the world as it is. The ability to conceive of the perfect is evidence that it exists.

Twenty: Unconscious Good

In order to retrain my intellect and find the heart's mind, I used the "Start with Heart" process (see page 77) to define, in systematic logic, what inspires me. I felt I had to prove that what changed and revived me made sense. I used this hierarchy— start with heart, free the mind, watch for fruit, and enjoy the process—to inform my mind how to make sense of troubling situations and to devise solutions, the success of which gave me great satisfaction.

Observing the unconscious: *Start with Heart* helped me capture my thoughts by reflecting on the previous day to find *heart* under activity on the topside. I looked for spontaneous unplanned activity; for unexpected mercy extended to me; for moments that excited my whole being. I was an explorer and a scientist trying to capture fleeting appearances of this natural good, to find its characteristics and intention. In journals, I captured raw reactions. In compositions, I put pieces together. I talked about what I found, whenever a friend would listen, and began to create language for what I saw.

The phenomenon, as a whole, was a surprise. It was a font that watered my soul, and a natural engine that put me at the helm, navigating my life with confidence about the nature of life and its good that supported me. There was substance and purpose rooted in some higher knowledge, and the evidence of that knowledge was in my involuntary, spontaneous responses.

Initially, I connected this to a sense of religious spirituality and faith in God, and how the eternal spirit is captured in the body. Then I took it further, to see the effect of the limitations of time and the cycles of life on the human spirit.

Eventually, I allowed for the fact that the spirit will be released from the body at death, released from time and from the physical. By separating the "electricity" from the "machine" I could see the differences between spirit and mind, between body and soul. The "electricity" is the life force in the body. It is there as long as I live. This life force is the eternal spirit immortal drawn to its ultimate destination, raising meaning in its wake. Spirit works in us as an unstoppable, self-renewing positive motivation. While in the body it leans toward God, the perfect good.

This life force resides in the heart and draws us body and soul, toward the good that exists as a part of life, a built-in characteristic as natural as the ground we walk on. When an unexpected event impacts life, the intellect loses the power to explain and control and to dictate; the heart naturally takes the lead. The very nature of spirit is transcendent, and pulls from the mind and body all the natural ability to overcome circumstance.

This is the *triumph of the human spirit* that is so inspiring.

Intuitively, we keep an unfailing and true course that adjusts to change; we are designed to survive. *Heart* appears in spontaneous, unplanned, unconscious sparks that instantly go to the mind and body, setting off a chain reaction where good ultimately wins over intellect. I call it "unconscious good" because the human will cannot accomplish it without the pure intention of spirit.

Twenty-One: The Cycle of Unconscious Response™

A series of actions carried out in a predictable sequence is a system, and when the same sequence repeats, it is a cycle. This cycle begins at the same point (intuition) and ends at its intended destination (an extension of good).

The 12 phases of unconscious response begin with the impact of an unexpected event. The moment the impact occurs, we instinctively draw from whatever intellectual and emotional resources we possess. There is no precedent, no box where we can calmly place the event with confidence in our ability to handle it. The unfamiliar is normalized within our self-culture where we have control. Our unique mix of internal priorities and self-government manages change and assures my survival as a person distinct from any other. Once the impact is absorbed within the self, our unconscious attachment to the process carries out change from its roots into the world around us.

Only an unprecedented unexpected event, one that causes a major emotional impact on a person's life, will trigger the first automatic unconscious response that initiates other responses. We unconsciously protect ourselves where we are most vulnerable: in the heart. By following the unconscious responses after many, many of these triggers, the sequence and its intended purpose eventually became clear to me. We process to overcome and, absorbed in the challenge, we may not realize that change from the heart is naturally inclined toward good.

These descriptions are an attempt to capture the characteristics of the phases and cycles I observed and recorded since 1997. I believe it is a natural phenomenon and, as such, I am interested in finding others who may have observed and studied the same kind of manifestations.

My theory is that this natural cyclical process turns the course of our lives gradually to keep the long-term progress in the direction of good. The automatic motion is a heartbeat that keeps the blood of human action alive with purpose and meaning. Like a study of gravity, we know its properties by its effect in the natural world. Unlike gravity, we observe the nature and design of the heart's mind in our unconscious responses to its presence. The ultimate effect extends into life gently and enlarges like ripples from a pebble tossed into a lake.

A Cycle of 12 Phases

The first six phases form a private internal process: From the moment of psychological impact an unconscious progression moves through our awareness, from an impulsive reaction to internal adjustment and then expression, and finishes in a personal breakthrough.

The second six phases manifest the change outwardly, and we unconsciously adjust to the reality of change that includes unconscious heart-satisfaction. Vestiges of the natural way of living before the change diminish and fall away, and a new good becomes permanent.

The only numbers used are one through twelve, beginning with unexpected change and ending with the adjustment toward good. Adjustment and growth continues, unfolding the way a plant moves from one stage of development to the next, with no abrupt end or beginning.

When we realize what unconscious responses tell us about our own hearts, we can choose to allow good to work within us—or we can work against good. There is always a cost of some kind, and we must be willing to accept the price good demands if we're to encourage our identity to mature so that our daily satisfaction in the pursuit of happiness increases.

Daily dis-satisfaction is the normal state for many people. It is the result of focusing on the inherent imperfection and entropy or decay of nature. An appreciation of good provides a natural stress reducer. Daily stress reduces in proportion to the level of our conscious awareness of good as an inherent trait of natural systems.

The pursuit of *intangible* happiness—the kind we feel in our hearts—is a challenge to our physical senses, our money-focused minds or pleasure-seeking bodies. Just as in taking on the disciplines of good health, following the heart's mind as a conscious choice rarely comes to the forefront except in cases of severe depression or disaster.

Part One: Owning Change

Phase One

A *first*: the unexpected impact of a new thing that instantly engages the whole being. It could be a major event, positive or negative, or simply new to a person. It could even be neutral except there are strong, impulsive thoughts and feelings.

The principle idea is that in Phase One we have no previous knowledge or experience to automatically contain the event. So, not understanding, we react intuitively and instinctively, from the heart, often with emotion. It is literally a knee-jerk response, unfiltered motions, words, or emotional outbursts that pop out before we think about it.

To see oneself raw and uncensored by the mind can be unsettling or embarrassing. However, it is very good information about the natural state of the heart at that moment.

Phase Two

Comprehension: Instinctively, we recover and pull ourselves together. Reason overcomes emotion and in a quick review of the experience we regain perspective, placing the new experience within an established set of priorities.

Spontaneous reactions are trimmed to support an ideal self-image, a composite of "self" that has already been building over time. This private conversation with ourselves forms a core identity that moves closer to an ideal, a standard and demeanor against which we want to be recognized. It is the source of personal, self-justified pride; a valuing of ourselves that does not rely on validation by others.

Phase Three

Having come to terms within, and from a place of personal identity, we look out again into the situation. We choose a position about how we want to relate to others, and to the situation as a whole.

Consider the impact of meeting a new employee at work, one who triggers an impulsive unpleasant reaction. It is automatic, and we may or may not know why we feel that way toward someone we just met. If our distaste shows, in phase two we would bring that uncharacteristic action under control. In phase three, we make an internal decision to manage interaction with that person; for example, we might choose a cooperative, professional manner if that's our normal approach.

As another example, say there's an unexpected death in the family or similar tragedy. In the shock, emotions are released; the mind loses its knowing composure. We may feel confused, overwhelmed with sudden grief. The immediate, unconscious response throws us off our confident pace in life.

In phase two, our priorities come to the surface. We may withdraw, go into action, comfort others, scream silently at God in anger, or thank God... We do whatever it takes to suppress the natural and overwhelming emotions with our preferred way to make sense of the world.

In phase three we choose a default position, one we will strive to return to as we work through the change. Maybe we know there will be times where we cross paths with a certain person or a certain occasion around the tragedy. We automatically use our self-imposed standards to guide us in preparing.

Phase Four

Now we enter life. Again. Now the situation is not new, and we have anticipated what may happen and how to keep our place. We walk out the choice; move into the new experience, picking our way through it, staying close to the unconscious guidance system newly formed in our hearts.

There's no script; we can't anticipate exactly what will happen and how others will behave toward us. But it is very important that we establish a place for the ordered self that works from the priority system that is unique to us. It is a matter of survival for the identity of this *self* to prevail. We navigate like a ship through coastal rocks, moving this way and that with a determination that flexes and yields, moving forward to the "shore" of our intention. Above the tragedy, among all the other persons involved we make the only place that can give us rest—one where we can be satisfied with survival.

Phase Five

Once the new has been managed and subdued we feel in control again. There's no need to monitor the change and life resumes, at least on the surface. Inside there's a settling, an assimilation. The new is integrated with what was before. The memory of the impact and the change we went through can be remembered, but life carries on as if it didn't happen at all. The unconscious retains the whole shift, and continues to work out its course.

Phase Six

Take a breath! In the unconscious, we sense a type of victory. The process of containing change and returning to equilibrium adds a new level of strength from within. We recognize that a barrier was broken, that we reached a new height of personal growth.

There's a display of activity, stemming from new confidence. It seems that there was only one barrier to full success, and it was broken. Eyes on a material goal of some kind, we press forward with new zest. It is the new sum of human strength, and we feel it.

Just as we feel the goal is within reach, just as we are about to collect the glory, the bottom seems to fall out. Like a dog on a chain we run at it with all our might and our energy is not diminished but try as we might, achievement has a limitation. There are no superhumans; we are all subject to the greater forces of life. The nature of nature is to urge us to improve, *and* to surpass our last best effort toward perfection.

Naturally, the mind stays on a tangible prize but perfect worldly success is imperfect. We never have it all, and spirit will inform the mind through disappointment.

Part Two: The Good Heart of Life

The first six phases are within the unconscious, a natural way of processing change. It is the work that prepares us to recognize and receive the good that life that will hand back to us.

In the second six phases, a coupling with the good heart of life occurs. In the natural, the heart knows to find the "good-in-process" happening constantly in life. It's the kind of good so constant that we often take it for granted. But the initial work of good must happen in our own hearts before it can be manifest in life.

As we unconsciously and spontaneously react to unexpected change, and subsequently re-orient and return to a familiar equilibrium, the breakthrough is part one of the good we receive. We process the unfamiliar good unconsciously; we literally *incorporate* it. It's a dance between spirit and soul that is slight in the mind but then the good begins to move outward from the heart, yearning for the fruit at the end that completes its life cycle.

In the second six phases, the heart redirects the intellect away from the self where its attention is on what the self can control. The heart has larger intentions, and its strength holds intellect and body in its grip. The self is only part of the heart's agenda now. In the good heart of life it becomes possible to establish our identity beyond the self, beyond *human* vision. The *real* intention of perfect good is for my life and my purpose to be joined with the rest of humanity. In the second six phases, out of the richness of the new private good, the heart moves outward toward good that can matter to others. Through the first six phases, good transforms our strength until it nestles in our hearts and then the good heart of life brings others toward us.

~~~

Phase Seven

For humans, spirit is a greater strength than mind or body. Life sets out to prove that in our experience. In the seventh phase our human strength is restrained, ineffective. If we look with the heart's eye, in the work where we are held back something comes to us. While we are powerless and ineffective in willfully applying ourselves to our goal, life adds to it, nevertheless, taking us further without our effort.

When we see benefit added to our lives exactly where we were working, there's a tendency to take the results as a product of our own effort. But the truth is that with the impact of change, our life was indeed turned at the heart. Now, in the limitation of our human strength, the intended good takes the lead.

Remember that I was consumed with this study, following the trail of unconscious good that was greater than me. So when I first saw this phase, it was from my heart's eye. I felt as if I were bound and gagged in terms of what I could affect. So all I could do was watch. As I watched, life moved the chess pieces of my game and I realized that it was not my game but that there were forces at work *for* me.

In phase seven, the exterior of life is brought in line with the place that change had brought to my heart. I became fixed in right relation to the unconscious good and my sight was adjusted so that I looked toward the good that naturally grew, nurtured by the forces of life.

Phase seven puts us in a new position, inwardly and outwardly. Our outer world becomes aligned with the corrected inner reality. A subtle change tells us we're not in charge; that no one ever really is. We're pointing toward a better, more accurate view where heart and mind have come together even if unconsciously.

Phase Eight

Now we're ready to enter life again, to begin again. The heart is revved up but we're not quite fully ready for what's to come. Like a baby in the birth canal, we continue to develop and fully realize the change. Life shifts around us; pressure increases and we're not moving forward or backward.

It's a unique place of realization, phase eight. Still feeling the familiarity of the place we left, there's discomfort not knowing what's ahead in the direction we now face. It's the liminal experience, in a doorway between two rooms. Not in either place, but one is before us and one is behind.

In the heart—if we see with our heart's eye—there's a calm, waiting for nature to take its course. It is natural, after all. The forces in life are there to support us, confident in the way life begins and is truly sustained. For the human, that sustenance is in the heart.

Phase Nine

Finally, the time has arrived. There's a flurry of activity around the revealing. What we felt moving and growing in phases one through eight now materializes. In some ways we are surprised; we knew in our hearts that something was coming, but even we didn't know exactly what it would look like.

The emergence of a new thing, in reality, can cause mixed feelings. In the process of it coming forth, there can be a sense of struggle and confusion. In some of my deep personal healing, I could identify with phase nine as the feelings I had in the birth of my children: equal parts pain and joy. As I became accustomed to the natural process of discovering the joy and vitality of living in the ups and downs, those polar extremes lessened.

Not entirely unexpected because of the unconscious gradual development, suddenly having witnesses to this birthing creates excitement. This is a primary characteristic of phase nine, that what has been growing *under the hood*, as it were, is revealed in a thing or occasion that other people see.

Phase Ten

After the birthing, the arrival as a tangible reality concludes. We have a chance to assess what it is that's been put into our hands. We count its fingers and toes, so to speak, poke and examine to see what is the length and breadth of this thing. What is it like? We can make conclusions and judgments after the fact.

We may see surface regularities and subtle differences or nuance. Something as simple as sizing up a project after it's done prompts us to evaluate the quality of the thing as a whole. We can make conclusions about it. Maybe we recognize the relationship between the result and the process that brought it about. Sometimes this is apparent in a chain of actual events; sometimes it is a thing perceived only by the heart and would take reflection and effort to recognize its importance.

In phase ten there's a quality of a purely human authority: the power to judge. We can categorize and name new things. Now that there's completion and fullness, we can place the thing in relation to what is already known and in order. There's a big picture again, and this addition has expanded our sense of reality.

Phase Eleven

Before a change and our adjustment to its impact, life had cohesion of sorts. Change adjusts that cohesion to allow for new good to grow. Our comfort is sacrificed because a static life is not healthy, and if there is no health there is no growth.

The impact of change alters our reality. In phase eleven, the crumbling of what was there before is now complete. Like an eggshell that is discarded for the contents of the egg, the life as it was can be no more. It was a natural structure that kept us safe while good grew large enough to break free of the restraint. For humans it is natural to grow away from the mundane and create something fresh, something better, something closer to good.

The point of the cycle of life for humans is to manufacture or increase *good* so that the will to live and thrive is renewed. Good comes in increments, ever unfolding and never attaining *perfect* good but ever striving *toward* perfect good. The process of change in the heart renews our hearts as we shed the old and live in the new.

Phase Twelve

This increment of good has finished its work and stands solid. Phases one through twelve conclude, firmly establishing a good—an authority holding its place. It ratchets up one more increment of good to dominate over mere existence. This small new place of good has substance.

When the authority of a good is established in an area of the heart, we are healed there. This is a root—a vein—that, once healed, can bring nourishment and growth, strength and energy to the soul. It becomes a world of good, there in that space.

No matter how insignificant a healing in the heart may seem, the change is fruitful. It affects our minds, emotions and behavior. We begin to live differently in that area of concern.

Good is an authority over the heart's mind and it must yield. It *wants* to yield to good. Once established, good is a power in the heart that transforms us, empowering mind and body where we follow the path of good.

Using analogy helps understand the 12 phases idea because 12 is common in the tools we use to track time. The calendar is one such tool, and the seasons as sections of a year. We can agree that we exist together at any point in time. For example, we can agree that it is Thursday, March 1, 2018.

The 12 months of the year can serve as a framework to see each of the 12 phases as part of the whole cycle of unconscious response. A clock can illustrate the passing of each phase in the whole of 12 hours. We can see half a day and each of the hours, all at once, just as we see each month as part of a whole year. Once we pick up the natural rhythm of the cycle, we can apply the appropriate principle to any point in time. In every sequence following the impact of an unexpected or unprecedented event, the principles of the 12 phases do their work internally, like clockwork.

One way to enlarge perspective is to see where you are in the natural human lifespan. In the following illustration, a lifespan of 120 years is divided into sections of 12 years each. The theory applies a principle of unconscious response attributed to each phase in the sequence. By dividing our lifespan into segments of 12 years each, it becomes a tool to help us reflect on the past and the future as part of a whole.

When we appreciate time as unfolding in 12-year phases, time seems to be passing very slowly. By returning again to the present, each day like today again seems to pass quickly. By expanding time in this way we can stand back and remove ourselves from the pressure of time. In one view, time is short; in another, we can feel the unfolding pace of nature in our own lives.

The 12 Phases Over a Lifespan: The Big Picture

Phase One: A new beginning – Birth to Age 12

Phase Two: Sort by personal priorities – Age 13 to 24

Phase Three: Choose a position in the new – Age 25 to 36

Phase Four: Anchor a position outwardly – Age 37 to 48

Phase Five: Return to control; perspective – Age 49 to 60

Phase Six: Expansion of personal strength – Age 61 to 72

Phase Seven: Aligned with spirit – Age 73 to 84

Phase Eight: Look forward accurately – Age 84 to 96

Phase Nine: Visible proof of spirit – Age 97 to 108

Phase Ten: Judge the result – Age 109 to 120

Phase Eleven: The former falls away – Death

Phase Twelve: The new is permanent and good – Eternity

A Year Unfolds in 12 Phases

Phase One: A new beginning – January

Phase Two: Sort by personal priorities. – February

Phase Three: Choose a position in the new – March

Phase Four: Anchor a position outwardly – April

Phase Five: Return to control; perspective – May

Phase Six: Expansion of personal strength – June

Phase Seven: Aligned with spirit – July

Phase Eight: Look forward accurately – August

Phase Nine: Visible proof of spirit – September

Phase Ten: Judge the result – October

Phase Eleven: The former falls away – November

Phase Twelve: The new is permanent and good – December

Conclusion

The heart has an uncanny connection to the intangible world of good. We express our hearts on the surface by voicing our thoughts, touching those we care about, showing up or staying home, moving objects to build or destroy; laughing, crying, dancing, working out. All this activity has a connection to the heart that knows more than the mind can conceive, more than the soul can feel, more than the body can accomplish.

If we know our hearts—the unconscious desire for good in all things—mind and body can work in a positive direction and life can be more satisfying because life supports progress over time. When we are alive in spirit, the heart sends that living force out into our words and actions. Heart is the difference that wakes us up out of slumber, out of the dullness of survival.

The real intention of good through the heart's mind is about the permanence of ideal, of the attraction of perfect good. We'll never have a perfect good on Earth, but we get these little deposits of perfect good every year, every day, every moment. But it is so slight; a breath, like breathing is to the body. The breath of perfect good is life to the spirit.

Watching my own manner of processing change showed me good was there; hidden, not absent. I came to believe it, and then trust it, and finally, to live in it.

Reflecting on the fact that we are creatures of this whole world, and just as there is an environment provided for the sustenance, protection, and preservation of animal society, this world is created and operates as it does for the provision and protection and continuity of humanity—according to higher purposes than ours.

The heart's mind is a challenge to our humanity because following our hearts will disrupt everything we have constructed with our own hands. But it is a privileged space where the heart thinks and gives an ability to see rightly. The challenge is to be willing to let the heart's mind instruct our intellect, emotion, will, and work.

The practice of starting with heart (respecting our cultivated impulses), freeing our mind (looking beyond the material world into the heart's mind), watching for fruit (accepting pieces of the dream as they come), and enjoying the process (joining in life's progressive flow) is something we can all embrace and live. It is our shared inheritance, our natural design.

With open hearts and enduring patience many friends let me find words to express what I saw with my heart's eye. They allowed me to see my thoughts from their perspective and to conceive of publishing a book. In Oregon Joy Denison has been a constant support in the development of published materials about my work. We have explored *The Cycle of Unconscious Response*™ from opposite natures and a common faith, comparing application and results since 2011. Joy's encouragement helped me produce a small book for Kindle in 2012, "Time and Life Cycles: The spirit's journey through time."

Honest commentary by those who reviewed the book drafts was critical to developing fullness of thought and greater satisfaction in writing. My writer son Evan Martin could speak to the craft of effective writing. Ever practical, my daughter Carrie Erickson challenged me about the direct relevance of the abstract ideas. Colleague and friend David H. Lee saved me from publishing a work that was too safe to be effective. And artist/editor/friend Maria Battista added a nice polish on the book's structure. Others gave their input and reactions that helped the book evolve to reach my audience more effectively.

Two insightful professional counselors, Valerie Montgomery, LPC, Beyond Beautiful, and Sandra "Jean" Parcher, LPC collaborated with me to publicly air my ideas in a yearlong project called "Unconsciously Good" from November 2014 to October 2015. Purely amateur broadcasting, we simply recorded and shared with subscribers unscripted conversations about *The Cycle of Unconscious Response*™.

There were a few who actually explored their own process of unconscious response with me: Uyen Tran Adams (now an experienced RN), my visionary sister Susan DeHerrera, and with the greatest attention, Joy Denison. With endless patience and goodness an old friend David A. Smith helped me find the first words out of my deep searching. There are friends whose feedback about *The Cycle* helped more than they know: Renee Sokoloff, Linda Friend, Wendy Carter, Rosemary DeHerrera, Darleen Daniels, Susanne Pyle, Summer Weisel, and Susan Edwards. In the entrepreneurs' gallery: Web site building leader Ben Wehde with *UnleashU*, videographer Anthony R. W. Lopez, and start-up strategist Jim Wittenburg.

The metamorphosis during the years at Colorado Mesa University (formerly Mesa State College) was under the guidance and freedom-giving encouragement of my instructors: In art and design, Carolyn Quinn-Hensley; drawing and painting, Joshua Butler; art advisor Deborah K. Snider; Dr. Steven Bradley in his passion for art history; the exacting English professor and writing guide, Dr. William Wright. The presence is missed of two excellent instructors who have passed away: Dr. Gordon Gilbert, who brought his love of physics to art and insisted I come to his mind-bending class, and professor of anthropology Dr. Barry Michrina who knew that, if done correctly, my study of artists as a culture would change me—and it did.

As a journalist and ethnographer I was compelled to capture instinctive words of wisdom spoken by artists and entrepreneurs. I found my own artist heart through interviews with such artists as John Anglim, Aimee Bourget, Malcolm Childers, Tish Collins, Cindy Holst, Jim Miller, Jan Roberts, and Mark Sonmor in Grand Junction, Colorado, whose works and spirit were the subject of my capstone thesis project in 2008. In Colorado Springs: Ellen Brown, Juel Grant, Liz Lata, and Douglas and Mallori Rouse are subjects of an in-process documentary about local artists.

The wisdom of Juel Grant, Maria Battista, Nora Hardin, Wendy Carter, Kris and Liese Chavez, Tracy Miller, Cass Mullane, and Chris Tatrn helped me acclimate to the Colorado Springs art community. In my travels for the beautiful *Colorado Journeys* magazine, published by the intrepid Kat Rhein of Western Colorado, I enjoyed the gracious attention of artists Frances Dodd and Allan McConnell, Dan Masimer, James Vilona, John Wilbar, and numerous artists from Denver to Trinidad.

Over the years health and mindfulness practitioners stepped in to sharpen me in body, mind, and soul, each one amazing and unique in their respective practices: chiropractor Bruce Davis for cranial specific therapy, Barbara Leach for intuitive Rolfing, Yolanda DelHierro for craniosacral and brain integration therapies, and Susan Blue for somatic therapy.

Some of the toughest critics and staunchest supporters are my family. Their love and concern have been lifelong and constant, with all the ups and downs that form the undergrowth and nurturing of life: My daughter Carrie Martin Erickson and son Evan Martin; my grandchildren Keegan, Blake, Kendra, and Ryder and his family; my sisters, my sister-in-law and my brother, with all their families, and the special mentorship and encouragement of my kindred-spirit aunt, Marylouise Tate.

Each person made an indelible impression on my heart from an inimitable being and unique perspective. I am thankful for every positive and negative experience that connected me to the whole of humanity.

APPENDIX

A Personal Chronology of Influential Books

The frontier of the mind is a *deep*, like the ocean. Exploring it requires a bit of bravery and a lot of support on the surface. I drew breaths from the heart and soul that these authors sent out to their readers. They are real people holding signposts that told me, "You're on the right track. Keep going!"

This reading list is only part of the philosophical, spiritual, practical, and health-supporting writings that opened my eyes to all the riches of knowledge that surround us. These and so many other talented and inspiring writers and leaders helped form the launching pad for my way of life as a heart-driven, organically sensitive worker.

(The list is organized by the year I read the books, not by their published dates.)

1991

The Gulag Archipelago, by Alexandr Solzhenitsyn (partial reading).

> Comment: This dramatic story by the Nobel Prize novelist and historian Alexandr Solzhenitsyn is based on his and other prisoners' experience in Stalin's forced labor

camps. What inspired me most was the way Solzhenitsyn kept mind and spirit alive while in captivity, in a cell barely bigger than his own body. Freedom of the mind is the very soul of identity.

The 7 Habits of Highly Effective People, by Stephen R. Covey.

Comment: Covey's work changed the whole context of success, away from time management and goal obsession toward personal development that moves from private victory to interpersonal and public victory.

2001

Starting From Scratch: A Different Kind of Writers' Manual, by Rita Mae Brown

Comment: I'm not a fiction writer but I took tips from her about interviewing to understand character. Unlike most writers' guides, this one had as much to do with how writers live as with mastering the tools of their trade.

Kosher Sex : A Recipe for Passion and Intimacy, by Rabbi Shmuley Boteach

Comment: This book was important in rebuilding my hope in one of the essential joys of living: a love relationship. Rabbi Boteach wisely divides the worlds of love and sex, and then brings them together again. His book turned my heart to the hope of a real love experience, one where sex is based on love, trust, and real intimacy – "kosher" sex.

2002

How to Think Like Leonardo daVinci: Seven Steps to Genius Every Day, by Michael J. Gelb.

> Comment: I loved the whole book. My favorite tool: Learn the Rules of Mind Mapping, "the rhythm of incubation." (Page 177) I used mindmapping software for years afterward.

Do It! Let's get off our buts! A Guide to Living Your Dreams, by John-Roger & Peter McWilliams

> Comment: I used this book for an exhaustive review of my abilities and dreams. "You can have anything but you can't have everything" helped me focus on my unquenchable desire to write. Some of the quotes are incredibly focused:

Nothing contributes so much to tranquilizing the mind
as a steady purpose – A point on which the soul
may fix its intellectual eye.

Mary Wollstonecraft Shelley (1808-1851)

One doesn't discover new lands
without consenting to lose sight of the shore
for a very long time.

Andre Gide, Nobel Prize, 1947

The Ultimate Six Sigma: Beyond Quality Excellence to Total
Business Excellence, by Keki R. Bhote

> Comment: Once I was out of the corporate arena, I was
> interested in keeping current with business trends and
> the evolving culture. I took note when the winds shifted
> more toward the human aspects of business. I retained a
> respect for the best leaders in the business world, like
> Stephen Covey ("7 Habits of Highly Effective People), and
> those speaking out about true quality in operations:
>
> "The thrust of the Ultimate six sigma is to take excellence
> beyond product quality: to excellence in customer loyalty
> – not just in customer satisfaction; to excellence in
> leadership – not just in management; to excellence in a
> nurturing organizational infrastructure; and to excellence

in releasing the inherent creativity of employees to reach their full potential."

- Robert W. Galvin, Chair of Board, Motorola

The Consultant's Calling: Bringing who you are to what you do, by Geoffrey M. Bellman

> Comment: I gained a lot of comfort and confidence in Bellman's recognition and affirmation of the relaxed productivity of the consultant's lifestyle. It was my natural tendency and I recognized that this would always be my default way of working, especially as a writer.

2003

Letting Your Life Speak: Listening for the voice of vocation, by Parker J. Palmer;

> Comment: Palmer's work, as with any philosophical or spiritual work, lacks the intellectual, physical motivation in which workers live. Palmer's language is firm, direct, real, and unassumingly confident. His confidence, as mine, comes from experience, searching, learning, and the inner processing of them all. We have discovered infallible meaning of life, the same truth, found without regard to the path to get there.

To reach workers I must speak their language. Heart is absent from education, from work, and subsequently, from life; "heartless" describes the result. My material speaks of heart in an intellectual manner.

Crucial Conversations – Tools for Talking When Stakes Are High, by Kerry Patterson, Joseph Grenny, Ron McMillan, and Al Switzler

Comment: I followed the authors' newsletter for a while where they advised on particular situations, both personal and business. I still refer to and recommend the tools taught in this book.

Because my personal guidance system was based in following my heart, their "start with heart" focus matched my own. Here's a quick reminder based on their advice, which I made to post on my refrigerator and still use:

Crucial Conversations ©
Start with Heart:
What do I really want for myself?
What do I really want for others?
What do I really want for the relationship?
How would I behave if I really wanted these results?

(The Third Option)
1.	Clarify what you really want in a conversation.
2.	Clarify what you really don't want in this conversation.
3.	Combine the two into an and question: How can I have _____ and _____?

2004

Four Kinds of Chance, by James H. Austin

Comment: In exploring "Chance IV" Austin illustrates how events that are supposed to be random might actually be the result of personal interests, lifestyle, and behavior of an individual. He suggests that a person could cultivate a natural environment where discovery can be expected to arise out of its unrelated and uncontrolled elements.

Austin describes occasions of "unintentional but subtle personal prompting of chance" that sounds similar to my experiences of "luck." I have a habit of stopping at the point where others naturally tend to think is the obvious direction to go. If I am not able to take action right then, I let go of that choice.

As a result something I never would have conceived of unfolds before my eyes. Finding these outcomes far more intriguing, I keep myself in check just to see what might occur. I often find that what comes to me is bigger and easier than anything I might have worked to accomplish.

2004 was a year of great change as I realized my financial predicament from a failed business, and went back to college. I explored a range of topics and did research on the psychological factors causing my family dysfunction.

2005

Drawing on the Right Side of the Brain, by Betty Edwards.

Comment: A revolutionary way of seeing what you draw. It removed huge barriers in my mind and I began to accept my natural ability to draw.

Do What You Love—The Money Will Follow: Discovering your right livelihood, by Marsha Sinetar

Notes from my journal: *I am moving gingerly forward, making sure I don't make any big leaps because this is sooo good! The chapter "Treating yourself as if you count"*

validated the things I have been doing. It affirmed the
authority I have been taking over my life to do what I think
should be done. I think this sensation is what's called
standing on my own two feet—even if no one else
recognizes it as such.

2006

The Human Condition, by Hannah Arendt

> Excerpt: "The new always happens against the overwhelming odds of statistical laws and their probability, which for all practical, everyday purposes amounts to certainty; the new therefore always appears in the guise of a miracle. The fact that man is capable of action means that the unexpected can be expected from him, that he is able to perform what is infinitely improbable. Again this is possible only because each man is unique, so that with each birth something uniquely new comes into the world..." (pp. 176-178)

The Artist's Way: A spiritual path to greater creativity, by Julia Cameron

> Comment: This book was very enlightening as I learned the work of an artist.

2008

The Four Agreements : A practical guide to personal freedom, by
Miguel Ruiz.

> Comment: So many people have mentioned this book and
> I'm glad I read it.

Essay on Man, by Alexander Pope(1688-1744)

> From "Epistle IV: Of the Nature and State of Man with
> respect to happiness":

>> "God loves from whole to parts: but human soul
>> Must rise from individual to the whole.
>> Self-love but serves the virtuous mind to wake
>> As the small pebble stirs the peaceful lake;
>> The centre mov'd, a circle strait succeeds,
>> Another still, and still another spreads;
>> Friend, parent, neighbour, first it will embrace;
>> His country next; and next all human race;
>> Wide and more wide, th' o'erflowings of the mind
>> Take ev'ry creature in, of ev'ry kind;
>> Earth smiles around, with boundless bounty blest,
>> And heav'n beholds its image in his breast."

A Whole New Mind: Why Right-Brainers Will Rule the Future,
Daniel H. Pink.

> Comment: In 2008 I met with the panel of overseers for
> my capstone thesis that included professors in
> anthropology and writing and my advisor in the art

department (Dr. Barry Michrina, Dr. William Wright, and Deborah Snyder MFA, respectively, Colorado Mesa University in Grand Junction, Colorado). The panel advised me about my capstone project—a book in allegory based on field research about artists as a culture, personally designed and printed.

Following the meeting, my art advisor asked if I had read "A Whole New Mind." I had not. She recommended I read the book saying that my talk in the defense of my capstone sounded very much like Daniel Pink's ideas. He became one of my favorite authors. I also read his books, "Drive: The surprising truth about what motivates us," and "To Sell is Human: The surprising truth about moving others." Daniel Pink is a researcher who writes about the major shifts in work culture.

2009

My Stroke of Insight: A Brain Scientist's Personal Journey, Jill Bolte Taylor

Comment: I was astonished to find that my emergence from deep introspection and rebuilding my mind from the heart to the world again was so similar to the author's journey.

Jill Bolte Taylor was a 37-year-old Harvard-trained and published brain scientist when a blood vessel exploded in her brain. With the eye of a curious neuroanatomist, she watched her mind completely deteriorate whereby she could not walk, talk, read, write, or recall any of her life. Because of her understanding of how the brain works, her respect for the cells composing her human form, and an amazing mother, Jill completely recovered her mind, brain and body.

Conscious Femininity: interviews with Marion Woodman.

Comment: A good description of my experience in becoming well.

"Life moves in cycles, consciousness expands. Each time we are faced with some new truth about ourselves part of us dies and a new part is conceived...points of transition where we are called to stretch into new maturity are the points where the addiction is most liable to resurface."

(Pp. 50-52)

How to Survive and Prosper as an Artist: Selling yourself without selling your soul, by Caroll Michels.

> Comment: I could not consider having a career as an artist, but through this book I learned how to help artists work out a business from their artist's heart. It's a difficult thing to put creativity above cash flow, but what is an artist if not a person of that demeanor?

2010

Permission Marketing: Turning strangers into friends, and friends into customers, by Seth Godin.

> Comment: Seth Godin is known for revolutionary ideas, simplified. His book titles often become catch-words among entrepreneurs, titles like "Tribes" and "Lynchpin," or this catchy statement in *Permission Marketing*: "America's favorite radio station is WII-FM (what's in it for me)." (p.225)

The Art of Loving, by Eric Fromm

> Comment: More help in deep self-discovery from the famous psychologist. Fromm writes about loving from the capacity of a fully developed personality, and from a

desire to give out of a productive lifestyle.

Five Minds for the Future by Howard Gardner

> Comment: A study of different perspectives within the mind: disciplining, synthesizing, creating, respectful and ethical. "These minds allow you to see every opportunity from multiple viewpoints and help you discern the best way to proceed to get the most from the circumstances."

The Fine Art of Small Talk, Debra Fine

> Comment: How and why it is that honesty and openness work.

2011

The World Is Flat: A Brief History of the Twenty-first Century, by Thomas L. Friedman.

> Comment: A nice summation of the transformation by the Internet, how we can see from here to China without obstruction. Communication technology puts people from different parts of the world in the same room.

The Next 100 Years: A forecast for the 21st Century, by George Friedman.

Comment: The rhythm of history is that the unexpected happens. Plan for it.

Outliers: The Story of Success, by Malcolm Gladwell.

Comment: "Outlier" is a term in statistics for the oddball point that deviates from the norm. When we see it in graphs we tend to disregard the outlier as irrelevant. But Gladwell uses stories of the amazing people who changed history *because* they were outliers. Gladwell says that on average it takes 10,000 hours or 20 years to perfect the unique character of outlier performance.

Trust agents : using the web to build influence, improve reputations, and earn trust, by Chris Brogan and Julien Smith

Comment: Brogan and Smith brought their online world to print, providing a catalyst to fuse my business mindset with the Internet culture and society. By drawing the human parallel between business behavior offline, with business behavior online, *Trust Agents* made it possible for me to easily update all my approaches at once.

Chris Brogan used media foreign in the tech culture—print—to bring his blogging success to traditional readers like me. A champion of the closet superhero, Brogan's classic style comes through in other books like, "It's not about the tights: An owner's manual for bravery" and "The Freaks Shall Inherit the Earth: Entrepreneurship for weirdos, misfits, and world dominators."

I loved being mentored online by Chris Brogan. For me, his was practical encouragement and humanized tools for emerging from obscurity. Backed by Chris and his spirit, I took a chance bringing my "freak" to the public via a website, a newsletter, and in magically showing up in the electronic world.

I'd rather be in the studio!: The artist's no-excuse guide to self-promotion, by Alyson B. Stanfield.

Comment: I had to move away from artist guides after reading this because it wasn't for me. It was for me to help artists. In general I know that artists are like writers and other creative people: we are independent and must work things out our way.

2012

Drive: the surprising truth about what motivates us. Daniel H. Pink.

Comment: I'm a fan of Dan Pink. He's a researcher whose

facts you can rely on. In *Drive*, we learn about the shift in jobs to the knowledge worker. Once basic needs are met, more money does not motivate the knowledge worker. We need freedom to move in personal strengths and be supported by rewards and an environment conducive to creativity.

Reference to Peter F. Drucker:

"Drucker coined the term 'knowledge worker' and forsaw the rise of the nonprofit sector, and was among the first to stress the primacy of the customer in business strategy. ...signaled the next frontier: self-management. With the rise of individual longevity and the decline of job security, he argued, individuals have to think hard about where their strengths lie, what they can contribute, and how they can improve their own performance."

Flow: The Psychology of Optimal Experience: Steps toward enhancing the quality of life, Mihaly Csikszentmihalyi

Comment: Mihaly has a wonderful ability to describe exactly how a person moves into a natural state of individual competence in natural talent. It is a feeling of flow, a detachment from the world in a focus and desire so clear that nothing can distract you.

I am always excited when I remember this book because it confirmed my deepest awakening when discovering the life of the unconscious mind. The organic way of producing and creating comes straight from the heart, as Professor Csikszentmihalyi says. It is "the ability to derive moment-by-moment enjoyment from everything we do." (Page 8)

Another great book by Csikszentmihalyi: *Good Business: Leadership, flow and the making of meaning*. He connects entrepreneurship with soul.

The Dream Society: How the Coming Shift from Information to Imagination Will Transform Your Business. Rolf Jensen

Comment: Really great verbalization of how the old business patterns don't work now and how to get used to uncertainty. Moves from Henry Ford to Bill Gates and Steve Jobs; from necessity to efficiency to creativity.

For Better or for Work: A Survival Guide for Entrepreneurs and Their Families, Meg Cadoux Hirshberg, columnist for *Inc.* Magazine.

Comment: It's always nice to get the feminine view, not leaving behind the importance of living whole. The organic way of working does not separate work and life like the artifice of the corporation does.

All entrepreneurs should commit to memory this important statement:

"When it comes to raising money, family and friends are the entrepreneur's low-hanging fruit. But the people who love and believe in us are also those whose fortunes we least want to imperil, and whose positive regard it hurts most to squander. Venture capitalists understand this, which is why they often prefer that the entrepreneur's friends and family invest before they consider a deal. As one CEO said to me, 'Venture c\people know you don't care about them, but that you'll work hard to make sure not to lose the money of loved ones.'" (Page 28)

2013

Body and Soul, A novel, by Frank Conroy

Comment: Breathtaking! Son of the working class who grows to become a piano prodigy.

Don't Make Me Think: A common Sense Approach to Web Usability, by Steve Krug

Comment: Brass tacks on the reading habits of Internet audiences.

Spontaneous Healing: How to discover and enhance your body's natural ability to maintain and heal itself, by Andrew Weil, M.D.

Comment: Singing to this choir! Health and heart knowledge tend to go hand in hand.

---

*Presentation Secrets of Steve Jobs: How to be **Insanely Great** in Front of Any Audience*, Carmine Gallo, Columnist, Businessweek.com

Comment: An analysis of the speaking method of marketing genius Steve Jobs, Apple computer founder. His style changed presentation history.

2015

The Biology of Belief, Bruce H. Lipton (Stem cell biologist and bestselling author)

Comment: Books like this exposed me to new ideas and pursuits in science relevant to my work regarding the human spirit and its visible effect on life. Lipton talks about his own discovery of "another 'mind'" at work, out of his control, "another (more powerful) force that was co-piloting my life." (P. 169)

I felt encouragement and a kind of camaraderie in work like Lipton's that went further on the same track I was on, messing about in the rooms of my own *deep*. "Occam's razor" and the heuristic approach to research brought credibility to my methods that are based on, but are not strictly bound to, the stringent methods of clinical science.

2016

Launch: An Internet Millionaire's Secret Formula To Sell Almost Anything Online, Build A Business You Love, And Live The Life Of Your Dreams, by Jeff Walker

> Comment: Very helpful, but the biggest takeaway for me is how his system is based on natural growth out of my community, my closest friends and associates.

Automatic Customer: Creating a subscription business in any industry, by John Warrilow (membership website model)

> Comment: Trends in business and marketing always interest me and the books available are endless. I like to

know where business is heading and it's fun to see how the principles that maintain its humanity always rise to the top. Local connection as a communication pipeline, a service, a convenience, and to improve quality of life stand as pillars that support the movements that follow technology.

What now? by novelist Ann Patchett.

> Comment: I enjoy Ann Patchett's fiction, and having been a relatively recent college graduate I found this book especially interesting based on her lauded commencement address at Sarah Lawrence College. I identify with her life as a writer, the staring into space as things try to gel, and her openness to the unexpected, "being open to the thing that actually winds up coming your way."

Anatomy of Love: A natural history of mating, marriage, and why we stray. Helen Fisher, PhD.

> Comment: As a holistic and organic being, I encourage inclusion of every element of living as part of the search for fulfilling occupation. Studies of ordinary experience

can be very enlightening. Fisher breaks down the architecture of human romance like an entomologist examines insects.

In recovering from the abrupt end of a long marriage, it was key for me to develop a non-reactive position toward the opposite sex. By identifying with men as just a variation of the same human as women, I found that the natural and healthy view was best. Nature's intention is that we complement each other, not oppose each other. Human nature wants the good and the beneficial.

As we support each other in being opposite, a fully mature man would ideally complement a fully mature woman, and vice versa. I have seen such occasions in real life, so it is my goal to let nature take its course; not in an animalistic way, but in the spirit of love—the human way.

2017

The Compassionate Samurai: Being extraordinary in an ordinary world, Brian Klemmer.

I read this book because my daughter was impacted so positively by the Klemmer leadership training. I found Klemmer's philosophy and principles to be as complete and effective a personal guidance as I've ever read.

Yes! 50 scientifically proven ways to be persuasive. Robert B. Cialdini. Author of "Influence"

> This is basically a book about sales, but through studies of human nature Cialdini shows the natural dynamics of how we work to benefit each other, and how we are wired to invite and provide benefit. As Stephen Covey's books elaborate, the best outcome is when everybody wins.

Unshakeable, by Tony Robbins.

> Comment: The ways of Tony Robbins, author, entrepreneur, philanthropist, and life coach mesmerize me, just as a study of full-on alpha male energy, working from roots of love. Because I took on a new career in finance to fund my future, and because my primary goal is to help people, I read this book to find a bridge between the financiers and us real people. It's not just about money.

Start with Why: How great leaders inspire everyone to take action, by Simon Sinek.

> Comment: Sinek's TED talks started a revolution of leaders who work harder to help others succeed by

finding their 'why.' Communicating our *why* is an infinitely more powerful motivator in a leader. It ignites the fire of our own passions when we hear what drives others.

Science in the Soul, Richard Dawkins

> Comment: Under his ranting criticism lie some nuggets, like: "...mysteries are all the more beautiful for being eventually explained. (Pg. 30)

Start something that matters, Blake Mycoskie

> Comment: The title says it all—very inspiring *and* make-it-simple practical.

The end of jobs, Taylor Pearson

> Comment: Pearson examines the historic change in the 20th century that transformed our ideas about working. If we create new work, we create more wealth. We can design a lifestyle of freedom that also benefits the world at large. Bringing to mind Csikszentmihalyi and Pink, Pearson lauds our natural inclination to grow and press

toward higher goals. Meaningful and valuable work makes capable and happy workers, and brings greater satisfaction in life.

2018

The Organic Entrepreneur: Cultivating the conscious capitalist, by Maxine Hyndman.

> Comment: Maxine put into words the exact spirit of the organic entrepreneur, the way I know and experience it. Every page fed my soul, in finding a true kindred spirit. The book elaborates on the experience of working from the inner being, out, in a way that is unique to each person. This is the very essence of my style in helping people achieve real satisfaction in working toward their dream life. The difference is, Maxine Hyndman has worked out the intricacies of letting a business be a true extension of a person's life and its cycles.

> There's no doubt that this author has lived the very life and all the challenges of an organic entrepreneur. Maxine eases the reader into a place of competence, working with the cycles of life to know when to work and when to grow.

The Naked Millionaire: A woman's guide to building a healthy relationship with money, by Maxine Hyndman.

> Comment: Maxine Hyndman wrote this book before *The Organic Entrepreneur*. I initially skipped over it, according to my natural aversion to focusing on money. But then I knew that Maxine would be taking her heart into the problems of money—and that she recognized that women might have an unhealthy relationship with money. This book has given me the connection I needed, to build "whealth," as she calls it, without selling my soul. She puts money in the right context for me.

About the Author

Elizabeth Diane Garcia Martin was trained in proper corporate structures which she adapted to the small business environment, focusing on workflow systems. She earned an interdisciplinary Bachelor of Arts degree in art and writing (graphic design, fine art, professional writing, and creative non-fiction) from Colorado Mesa University (formerly Mesa State College) in 2009. Elizabeth's continual work with entrepreneurs and artists brings insight to workers of all kinds to help them see who they are in what they do.

Elizabeth's desire for, and assurance of, a better future is excited by the knowledge that love will always win in the end. This certainty of good brightens her view of the future for her children, her grandchildren, and their children's children.

Elizabeth is a lifelong Coloradan and now lives in picturesque Colorado Springs.

Notes

Made in the USA
Monee, IL
16 April 2021